Before the Rooster Crows
A Journey through Faith

Zaria Hicks

3G Publishing, Inc.
Loganville, Ga 30052
www.3gpublishinginc.com
Phone: 1-888-442-9637

©2024 Zaria Hicks. All rights reserved.

No part of this book may be reproduced, stored in a retrieval system, or transmitted by any means without the written permission of the author.

First published by 3G Publishing, Inc. November, 2024.

ISBN: 9781941247471

Printed in the United States of America

Because of the dynamic nature of the Internet, any web addresses or links contained in this book may have changed since publication and may no longer be valid. The views expressed in this work are solely those of the author and do not necessarily reflect the views of the publisher, and the publisher hereby disclaims any responsibility for them.

Dedication

This book is dedicated to those who have helped me walk in the footsteps of Jesus.

To do so takes more than just good shoes.

To understand that Jesus died for us is more than just good news.

To not only identify, but target the issues, that plague Christians, aimed at dismantling the peace, freedom, family structure and very salvation we strive for. All while simultaneously dealing with the humanistic tendencies we struggle with as individuals to reach our full potential, can be quite daunting and even challenging at times.

To be a woman or man of honor, you must first understand the cost of your sacrifice and required obedience, deny yourself, submit to God, and then pick up your cross.

Especially, when called to function in a position where you not only sympathize but empathize with those with whom you will encounter when rebuilding broken lives and families, which inadvertently requires some exposure to your own life's journey as well.

Churches, pastors, ministers, mentors, and fellow Christians are placed strategically in positions as a means to glorify the God who brings liberty to the captive(s).

It takes women and men of integrity, whose prayer comes before their practice to actuate such an outcome.

Individuals who speak the truth in love without compromising their integrity or filter down the word of God.

Those who mourn with you through sad times, yet maintain their resolve to counsel, support or help you through strife, to edify your spiritual as well as personal growth, as both Christians and individuals.

Those who pray with you through trials and laugh with you through life.

"How beautiful are the feet of him who bring good news to men."

I want to say thank you to the pastors and ministers, friends, and family, who have strengthened me throughout my journey thus far.

I want to especially thank those Shepherds who have poured into me from the very beginning, feeding me with the words of truth and life so that I could grow and develop and understand what it means to be a woman of integrity and a woman of God.

To Pastor Bani Brown (my very first pastor), Pastor Isaac Hicks, Pastor Teddy Otobo-Sheriff, Pastor Albert Ortiz, Pastor Tammy Stradford (my counselor and mentor), Reverend Yvonne Stradford, Reverend Patricia Drayton, Minister Valerie Chase-Mason, Minister Luci Serrano, Pastor Johnson Bowie, and the many individuals who I have gleaned from through teachings and preachings.

I want to give a special thanks to my husband Terrence C. Hicks, who has always believed in me and encouraged me throughout the years, who, seeing my destiny years before it began, prayed for it to come into fruition. I love you immensely.

And, last but not least, to my children: Ricardo, David, Joshua, Leilani, Joel, Skylar, Eli and Karimah, all whom I love dearly and in their own individual way have contributed, challenged or deposited something in me that was pertinent to my growth as a mother, Christian and individual.

Thank you all.

Epilogue

Father, today as I drove in the car I began to reflect upon my life and my relationship with You and the things that I've witnessed and experienced this far in my Christian walk.

I had to admit, that despite being introduced to You in February 1990, there was still so much I didn't know about You, but You wanted me to recognize that so that I could develop my standing in You. That clarity is just becoming slightly more evident to me today. And it's not because You've withheld Your truth that it has been such a long time coming, but rather my own resistance to the truth of who You really are based on my perceptions.

Because I'm human, and in the flesh, I have mistakenly equated You to what I know and understand, rather than who You are and state to Be.

When I asked myself the question, *"Who am I,"* my immediate response should have been *a child of God*, but instead, my initial and immediate thought is *no one*. However, as the question festered in my mind, another thought entered: I am somebody! I am a mother, a wife, a servant, a cook, a provider, a listening ear, and a worshiper.

But God whispers softly to me, *"My child, those are things you do, not who you are. Who you are is the daughter of a king. Who you are is Precious to me. Who you are is loved by Me."*

I contemplated the thought. Am I more than just the sum of my parts? Somewhere within my broken pieces, I am whole in Christ.

Although I didn't realize it at the time, I was not relegated to others' perception of me, to titles, job positions or the criteria that the world around me requires for us to facilitate in order to complete the definition of self.

So often, I also questioned whether or not I had been gifted with talents and abilities that God could use in and through me. It is a curious thought. Inwardly, I had always felt that I was destined for greatness, and yet looking where I stood at the time made me cry. My opportunity seemed to have passed, and I was saddened my failed opportunities and squandered years as though my life was already over.

To acknowledge that I had gifts, also meant recognizing that those gifts have been God-given and placed in me on purpose, for a purpose. This would mean that I would have to concede that the Father foreknew me, and chose me deliberately; and that knowledge went against the feelings of rejection I experienced in the natural world, even as a Christian.

I had addressed my need for a Savior but hadn't progressed to accepting His grace for my life that said I was accepted, and called, and loved.

So, if I have been called, accepted, loved and given talents and abilities to fulfill God's plan and purpose for my life, what are my unique God-given gifts?

What were the talents that God had placed in me to edify His name that were without repentance or an expiration date so long as I had breath?

My friend, and fellow champion in Christ, understands that it is a very dangerous thing to be alive and not know God or His purpose for your life – that the lack of knowledge of knowing who He created you to be leaves you open and susceptible to too many variables, and allows a foothold for the enemy to try and deceive us regarding who and whose we are.

My purpose, our purpose, everyone's intended purpose, is to glorify God and enjoy Him forever. Now we know that this epiphany does not actuate itself on its own, and more often than not, so many graves are filled with unfulfilled purpose and potential that was never accessed.

However, no matter where I am today or as of right now, no matter what condition you or I find ourselves in at this very moment, if we are still here and God is relaying this message to us, we still have time to do His will. And if we are unaware or clueless as to what our calling is or where to start, we must beseech heaven because it is imperative that we discover the calling that God has placed on our individual lives.

Each of us would need to make a careful exploration of who we are and the work we've been given. If you want an idea of where you are going and the direction God is steering you toward, you must examine the roads and avenues most taken in your life thus far. What seems to be the resounding theme? What types of circumstances do you most find yourself responding and relating to?

I chuckle, slightly amused, because this is something I have both neglected to do and denied—once revealed—at varying points in my life.

Speak, bind up, cast out and loose!! Walk in your gifts so you can walk in the authority that you have been given by God. We, as children of the Most High, need knowledge of the word of God in order to operate in faith and understand His will for us and His people.

We also need wisdom to act according to God's purpose. Wisdom is a revelation of divine counsel so that we can see ahead the things God has prepared for us so that we may speak and direct accordingly.

We also need to understand that we'll never receive anything without being tested and tried to see if we are faithful and worthy, with proven integrity, to nurture our gifts and use them for God's glory.

Contents

Dedication	*3*
Epilogue	*7*
Introduction	*13*
Why Me?	*19*
Chapter 1: Faith in Process	*23*
Abiding	*29*
Chapter 2: A Measure of Faith	*33*
Trusting in God	*44*
Chapter 3: What Do You Do When Faith Dies?	*47*
I Shall Not Want	*55*
Chapter 4: The Clock Is Ticking	*59*
Lord, Help Me Let Patience Have Her Perfect Work	*64*
Chapter 5: Trust in God, Don't Fall Back on Cliches and Idioms	*67*
You're With Me, Even in the Lowest Valley	*72*
Chapter 6: What You Don't Know Can Hurt You	*75*
Why Worry When We Can Pray?	*82*
Chapter 7: Are You Nearsighted, Farsighted or Blind?	*87*
My Help	*95*

Chapter 8: The Faithless Believer	*99*
Help Me Remember	*106*
Chapter 9: Knowing is Not	
Half the Battle, It IS the Battle	*109*
He Will Give Me a Song	*116*
Chapter 10: It Doesn't Add Up	*119*
Thou Changest Not, but Your Method Does	*122*
Chapter 11: New Wineskin:	
Change Your Garment	*125*
Empty Me Out	*129*
Chapter 12: Don't "Go!"	
Your First Love is Waiting on You	*133*
Hope in God	*143*
Chapter 13: Be Like Thomas, but Don't	
Let Them Change Your Name	*147*
I Have Overcome the World	*155*
Chapter 14: Guard Your Heart!	*159*
What's In My Heart	*164*
Chapter 15: Change Your Mindset	*167*
Direction from God	*175*
Chapter 16: Sometimes You Just Have to	
Wipe and Flush	*177*
Rest in You	*185*
Chapter 17: The Other Side, A Journey	
Through Faith	*189*
Father, Direct Me	*201*

Introduction

When I met my God-ordained husband, I was at one of the lowest points in my life. And although this feeling/state of mind had become second nature to me, I was unaware that things as I viewed and perceived them were about to drastically be dismantled, challenged, and changed.

Once again, I found myself at the cusp of another divorce – emotionally, physically, mentally, and psychologically abused, and preconditioned by past circumstances and traumatic events. Life for me was proceeding as usual.

Yes, I was a Christian, but I lived by Murphy's law: "Whatever can go wrong will go wrong."

I was so tired of hope and expectation failing me, I decided it was easier not to "believe" for anything than to hope for something, only to be disappointed.

Ironically, I knew and believed in my heart God to be almighty, able to do anything, change any situation, heal the sick, move mountains, even raise the dead (if you will). Nothing was too hard for Him, and if you asked me, I would tell you just the same.

I was an encourager and I poured into people the hope and love of God; all while having my own broken cistern which could hold no water. (Jeremiah 2:13)

You see, I believed in God, and that He was able to do the impossible and the improbable, but when it came to me … well I just thought He didn't want to do it!

I was a failure, a sinner unworthy by my own standards.

I had failed at marriage. I didn't have a great relationship with my parents. My kids were rebellious and contrary. I had lost my job, and therefore my identity. I was struggling mentally and emotionally with issues of unworthiness and self-pity; and yet, I sat in church week after week, hearing the gospel, agreeing with the message and still rejecting its promises for my life.

How is that possible?

Writing this now it seems almost ridiculous; reading it most likely comes off as cynically oxymoronic. And still, it was my truth and secretly maybe yours as well.

The question remains: Why then practice something you yourself can't seem to believe?

The answer is simple: I wanted to believe that it was true and that I had something to hope for.

Truthfully, I knew that without God in my life I would completely implode. God is wonderful. He is so awesome in His nature and make-up there are truly no words that can adequately express how amazing He is. Even when you are at the bottom of yourself, He can lift the residue left in your broken, empty vessels, remold you and fill you to overflowing.

I began by saying that my husband came into my life during one of the darkest seasons of my life. During the time of a bitter and painful separation from an abusive spouse, I developed an unexpected friendship with a man that would become my champion.

As my closest friend and a fellow Christian, I felt safe talking to someone who wouldn't judge me or my past. So often Christians feel entitled to speak their opinion, mind, truth and conviction into the lives of other Christians as though they have arrived to some precipice elite, above the realm of failure and defeat. This is so dangerous, not to mention ungodlike when our position makes us think that we are equipped to judge others based on where we think they have fallen short.

Oftentimes we place people in a state of bondage and rob them of their freedom to even release the pain without feeling condemned. In fact, for many, many years of my life I lived a broken, battered, desecrated existence hidden behind a false smile and overcompensation of business in order to avoid the very life I was trying to live fully in Christ.

No one knew my innermost thoughts or deepest struggles, how I contemplated and attempted suicide more than once, in an effort to release myself from the pain that was so pent up and pulsating it overwhelmed me in droves of sadness and despair.

I couldn't share my inner ideations and experiences with Christians for fear of judgment, and I couldn't share them with non-believers for fear of creating a bad name for the God of my salvation. Therefore, I just sat mulling in it, wondering when the outlet would come.

So, you could imagine the weight that was lifted when I became friends with a person with whom I could share my whole truth. I began divulging my lifelong struggles of failed dreams, abuse, and rejection to the one true ear that was listening at the time … and his conclusion to the whole matter was absolutely astounding:

He considered me blessed! Blessed?

How in the world could he have taken that perspective?

Had he not clearly heard the things that I had been saying to him?

Was he not listening to all my tales of calamity and woe over the years of my life that I had experienced?

Could he not *see* the pain in my face, *read* the hurt in my eyes, or *hear* the pangs of my bleeding heart from all the ache it had endured?

At some juncture in one of our many conversations earlier on, he would even go as far as telling me that he was even jealous that God loved me so much, and at that point I thought he was insane.

How could he deduce that God, who had not only seen, but also allowed my every struggle, without intervening or changing the outcome of so many tragic, heart wrenching situations, loved me … me?

It seemed as though I was being ostracized, rejected, and punished for all my wrongdoings in this, and my past life. I was walking around like Hester Sue with a branded scarlet letter for all the world to see, judge and laugh at me.

In fact, whenever I would hear a preacher say: *"If it was just for you, Christ would have came and died;"* inwardly, I would think to myself, *"not for me."* I was convinced that though *"many are called"* (Matthew 22:14) ... *I wasn't amongst the "chosen," a*nd it was just a matter of time before I would be plucked out. (Matthew 13:24-30)

I smile at the thought now, but secretly I envisioned myself at the door of the church trying to come in (to salvation), while God had his foot on my chest trying to keep me out. Determined to convince my then friend (later to be husband) of what I believed was God's true opinion of me, I began relaying all my thoughts and conclusions, giving him what I believed was a summation that testified of how God had forgotten about me. Assuredly, he would come to see my point of view once I was able to lay out the complete picture of my whole worthless life. And when I did, he responded with five simple words that would forever change the course of my life from that point forward.

He said, *"What makes you so special?"*

He said those words not gently, not with caution, not guarded by the obvious pity party I was having for myself, but matter of factly, resolutely, and almost harshly. Immediately I became confused because it was such a contradiction to my thought process and state of being.

He continued, *"... What makes you so special that the word of God would apply to everyone else but you? Are you that important?"*

I was verklempt and speechless. It was so simple and yet so profound.

Was God a liar? Was He unfair? Was He unjust?

Did He have only certain people in mind when He spoke of grace, mercy, forgiveness, and His love? Or, was I so self-absorbed that I neglected to see how excluding myself from God's provision and truth completely nullified who I was claiming Him to be and who He truly was.

The revelation gave me a newfound hope I had not considered; an opportunity to thrive as I had when I first became a Christian and accepted Christ; because I suddenly understood how I had been willfully rejecting Christ's sacrifice at calvary, and I didn't want to be found guilty of that. But here's what you must understand – making a declaration does not make it so. Taking a stand to change because of new information received does not equate to immediate transformation.

Remember, *"The devil is as a roaring lion seeking whom he may devour."* (I Peter 5:8) John 10:10 describes him as *"a thief who comes to steal, kill and destroy."*

This destruction is not limited to the body, but more so directed at the mind. His underlying intention is to rob the word of God from your thoughts before they take root. His expectation is to destroy, or in the least obscure your vision of the truth (Proverbs 29:18) because if you can't imagine it, you won't believe it can come to fruition.

This means that in order to live victorious and free in my revelation of who Christ was to me and how God's love abounds toward me, I'd have to meditate on that word of knowledge I had received and regurgitate it daily. I would have to actively engage in renewing my mind by reading God's word to remind myself and rehearse the promises and hope God had in store for me. I would have to pray regularly and adjust my way of thinking, so that the negative thoughts would not regain a hold of my mind as a way to try and bring me back into bondage.

This would be why, metaphorically, my eleven-day journey to freedom would ultimately take years and years of going around in the same circle until I finally realized that my struggle with Christianity was not about God himself, but rather what I understood faith in Him to be.

Psalms 27:4-6 says, *"One thing I have desired of the Lord that will I seek: That I may dwell in the house of the Lord all the days of my life, to behold the beauty of the Lord, and to inquire in His temple. For in the time of trouble He shall hide me in His pavilion; in the secret place of His tabernacle He shall hide me; He shall set me high upon a rock. And now shall my head be lifted up above my enemies all around me. Therefore, I will offer sacrifices of joy in His tabernacle; I will sing praises to the Lord."*

Why Me?

Father,

I, like David, am often amazed at why You are mindful of me.

In Your verse's You speak about You being a good and faithful Shepherd who cares for the well-being of Your sheep.

It emphasized that Your rod and Your staff comfort me, and in my research, I came to understand that Your staff represented Your guidance and support.

That even the end of the staff was shaped in a way that helped to dislodge sheep when they were stuck or was used to lift them up when they could not help themselves.

Your rod, on the other hand (which was separate from Your staff) was not used for chastisement, but for protection against the enemies that would otherwise harm the sheep.

You prepared a table before me in the presence of my enemies to let them know that You had my back, that Your watchful eye was upon me.

You were taking up the responsibility for feeding me and caring for me.

Today, You remind me that I was made a little lower than the angels but crowned with glory and honor.

Oh, how precious we are in Your sight.

How much do You consider us, the workmanship of Your hands?

Father, in a world of so many, where sin and death and failure to acknowledge You, You are still mindful of me.

You, like a good Father, like a dedicated shepherd, closer than an unyielding friend, You are ever mindful of us, Your children, of me, Your child.

When I consider my life and my thoughts and my choices, I definitely don't understand how You could care so much about me, and yet You do! And not only mindful, but the thoughts that You think of me are high minded, considerate and purposeful.

Father, like any good parent You want me to succeed, because my success resonates Your goodness.

Help me Father to see myself as You see me.

Help me to remember that when I fall, You are not waiting in the wings to say I told you so, but instead, You are right beside me helping me back to my feet.

You don't want me to fall into the hands of my enemies, but rather You want them to know that You represent me, that You'll go before me and fight my battles and that in my deepest despair I am seated at Your table, and You are caring for me and strengthening me in the confidence that You will never leave me or forsake me and You want to get that word out to anyone who even thinks about coming against me.

I am Yours and You are mine.

Why me Lord?

I'll never understand it, but I know that if You said it, I need to believe it.

Amen.

Chapter 1: Faith in Process

Did you know that the word FAITH is said to be mentioned over three hundred times in various translations of the Bible?

As Believers and Christians, we use the word to solidify our reliance and alliance to God based on what we read and understand about Him. The Bible states, *"Now faith is a substance* (material or fabric) *of things hoped for and the evidence of things not seen."* (Hebrews 11:1)

In other words, faith is the main ingredient in the recipe of salvation. And *"He that comes to God must believe that He is …, for without faith it is impossible to please Him."* (Hebrews 11:6)

Acts 16:31 states, *"Believe on the Lord Jesus Christ and you shall be saved."*

Therefore, is God impossible to please without faith? Or are you?

The reason for this harsh imposition is because, if we toggle between two opinions, we can never fully trust God. How can one possibly please someone they don't believe in?

Allow me to pose a synopsis for you in order to make an analogy:

If you were a cake, would you consider yourself sweet, satisfying and fulfilling, or salty, bitter, and sour? Would you be satiating or leave people wanting for more?

We know there are several ingredients that go into the science of great cake making, which are made up of many small, intentional steps that altogether lend themselves to an intended outcome of deliciousness. Should one or more of those steps be missed or omitted, it will result in the failure of the perfection it was intended to be. Should anything be done out of sequence, the outcome will suffer, and, as a result, the end-product will not be as expected.

Consider now for a moment that each individual ingredient may or may not seem to bear any significance on its own, but rest assured without any one of them, the end-product will be affected. Our life's structure (our cake) is composed of a variety of components geared toward a successful, sound, luxurious outcome.

God is the master baker, and He knows how to proportionately measure every ingredient in our life to construct the perfect cake.

Flour is the major substance needed to create what is to become the cake. However, would one ever consider eating a cup (or two) of raw flour in the name of calling it cake?

It is dry, bland, tasteless, has no structure, and has nothing in and of itself to be desired alone; but if left out, it would cause the cake to be dense and thick, and in many cases leave the batter raw in the middle.

God is somewhat like our flour too, in that without Him we have no cake.

Nevertheless, in this scenario we are the flour, and without Him we have no substance. Without Him every other step is pointless. Without Him life is dry, bland, tasteless and has no structure.

He is the foundation and basis of any, and all things upon which we will indulge and build each ingredient.

We know that sugar is sweet, and yet without it a cake will lack flavor and taste bland. But did you know that too much sugar can weaken the structure of the cake so much that it cannot stand, and collapses?

Have you ever heard the saying, "You can never get enough of a good thing?" Yet, what we may perceive as "good" can often throw off a person's perspective of the world causing them to crumble under the pressures of life's challenges.

What about eggs? Have you ever considered what their purpose is exactly?

They provide the structure and richness that would otherwise not be there should they be omitted. They bind the ingredients together to make a stable product. However, if we left them raw, they could potentially pose a danger and cause severe food poisoning.

The eggs in our life are the substantial, life changing events that bring density, richness, and fullness to our overall experience. They bind together during fragile moments in our lives that otherwise become compartmentalized in our hearts and bring them all together to see the bigger picture.

Salt enhances the complexity, by bringing depth of flavor to each of the ingredients within the batter and balances out the sweetness. However, too much salt can overpower all of the other ingredients and render it inedible.

The salt provides the sweet, not only with richness, but balance. Everyone has experienced at least one salty person in their lives. Salty people are those people who react badly to a difficult circumstance – and excessive saltiness can make whatever it's added to unpalatable.

Have you ever experienced someone who is so complicated that their ability to see or believe anything outside of their own viewpoint and believes everyone else's is skewed?

The bible says people like those are good for nothing but to be trampled under feet or cast aside. (Matthew 5:13) In other words, the difference or impact that they could have made becomes lost and of no value; and what essentially happens to anything that's oversalted? We throw it away.

Baking soda and baking powder are leavening agents that help the cake rise to its full potential. At least one of them is essential to give the cake body, but most often these ingredients alone taste bitter and have no nutritional value.

Bitterness is described as the sharpness of taste and lack of sweetness. The dictionary defines bitter people as people who display anger and disappointment at being treated unfairly, further explaining that someone who is bitter is usually responding to, or defensive because, they have experienced difficulties in the past that they have not fully recovered from.

Sourness is related to the acidity level in the food, which stimulates digestive activity to help get rid of built-up waste; it is also unctuous and good for the heart. Nevertheless, sour people have the same reaction as an acid: they expect a harsh outcome, and often respond negatively in circumstances that were not necessarily meant to be that way. And as we know, too much sourness can quench the appeal of anything originally intended to be sweet (good) because like an acid, it eats away at the substance instead of enhancing it.

In fact, a true acid's primary function is to affect the prefrontal cortex area of the brain, the area which controls mood, thinking, reactions, panic, and perception.

Altogether, these components make for the best quality product once combined proportionately and appropriately, and yet individually could not produce anything reminiscent of a cake. As we consider each step, let us be end-goal minded. What is it we are seeking as the result?

These are all poignant happenings, folded into one; the good and the bad, that allow us to see God in the whole experience for His glory. But, if we fail to combine them appropriately, we can become tainted by the salmonella that each difficult, raw, life changing event can potentially add to our overall outcome.

Let's think of this concept in another way for a moment.

If you wanted to bake a cake and the recipe called for flour (because there are flourless cakes), and you put all the ingredients together according to the directions, but you choose to leave out the flour, you will not have your desired outcome according to the instructions because you chose to omit the main ingredient necessary to produce the product to its best result.

Therefore, the same is true for faith and salvation. Surely, if you believe in Christ, that He is the only Son of God and that He was resurrected from the dead and accepted salvation, you might be saved. However, you wouldn't be living as victorious of a Christian life as God intended for you if there were parts of salvation, or the Bible, that you chose to believe are not true or for you.

In fact, you might find that without faith, salvation grows flat.

Such is the way in our natural world.

Romans 8:27-28 states, *"And He who searches our hearts knows the mind of the Spirit, because the Spirit intercedes for the saints according to the will of God. And we know that God works all things together for the good of those who love Him, who are called according to His purpose."*

Therefore, as we sit in the oven (of life) let us consider the temperature by which we measure our surroundings, components and the events that have altogether made us who we are and who we are to be.

And while we are transitioning and transforming our individual lives through the qualities that add up to a more complex product, let us consider and measure the things we have responded to and held on to, allowing us to evaluate whether we are a well-balanced combination growing into our best end-product. God has and continuously does.

He carefully considers all of the facets, products and portions required to bring forth a beautiful end result intended to be divided amongst others, so that they can get "fat" off of the wholeness our experience will bring to them – for what good is a cake that cannot be shared?

Abiding

Father in the name of Jesus, I come to You today asking that You pierce my heart, that You wash my hands, that You cleanse every sin and every evil imagination, thought or deed.

Forgive me Father for failing and falling short of Your glory and giving You the honor in all things as is my reasonable service and calling for this great salvation that You have freely bestowed upon me without prompting or request.

Lord, before I understood my sin, You abolished its power and reign over my life as long as I choose to abide in You.

In reading Your word, I understand much more clearly what it means to abide.

You are asking me to rest, take comfort in, a-join, align, connect, engage, cede, and make You my home, hope, source, supply, resource, and lifeline.

These are my expectations.

These are my requirements.

I must choose to engage with You in purposeful ways that dismiss my will, desire, tendencies, and normalcy.

Father, to abide in You means to let go of everything that I know or understand to be what I deem or perceive my life to be based upon my ideologies, concepts, or resources.

Father, to abide in You means I abandon my will completely for Your plan for my life.

"If I abide in You and Your word abide in me" ...

Father that is a twofold command because for me to abide, stay within the guidelines, and please You, I need Your word of truth.

I need to know what it is You say and think about me, I need to seek out to attain and retain Your words, for They are Spirit, and they are life.

Your word is the pathway to godliness and holiness without which no man can see You.

It's like a fruit growing on a tree with seeds that are copying Your DNA to reproduce what You are causing me to become.

Abiding means trusting in You and not veering on my own.

It is the image of Christ in us, the hope of glory.

It's the equivalent to being sustained by the God that houses, nourishes and gives us life.

Father, help me to abide, always, in every season, situation and circumstance.

Help me not to let go of Your unchanging hand, even if I feel as though sometimes my resources have dried up.

Help me to remember that *"in due season, I will reap, if I faint not."*

Father help me not to look from without, but to look within to those things that You have already provided, and made provision and accommodation for.

Everything else is a false vine.

Everything else in this life is geared toward using my resources, which are limited and dry up.

Father, I want to draw from the only source that is able to sustain me and help me to grow gracefully without any threat to how much I can glean, how long I can draw and how "fat" I can become within who You are.

You are the one immutable God and *"under Your wings I shall trust."*

Thank You for teaching me to abide so that I can thrive.

In Jesus' name I pray.

Amen.

Chapter 2: A Measure of Faith

As Christians, we rely on faith as a foundation of our belief. In fact, without faith the basis of our position would be pointless and void of the ability to build thereafter. Therefore, it behooves us as Believers to understand exactly what having faith means.

Miriam Webster Dictionary defines "Faith" as:

1. complete trust or confidence in someone or something.

2. strong belief in God or in the doctrines of a religion, based on spiritual apprehension rather than proof.

Now, as I see it, many of us follow the second definition more closely than the first. I mean, at a glance, we recognize that to some degree we all have an understanding of who God is based upon some doctrine of teaching we may have received or encountered. It is also reasonable to suggest that our faith is based on the unseen, rather than tangible proof.

However, if we were to delve deeper into the true meaning of faith, which is more closely related to the first definition, we may find it more difficult to conceptualize the idea in a way which grasps the entirety of its meaning, in such an effective way that it leaves no room for doubt or questioning.

The truth is, to define faith as complete trust in God may leave holes and gaps exposed on all our behalf when standing on the outside looking in.

Miriam Webster Dictionary defines "Trust" as:

1. a. assured reliance on the character, ability, strength, or truth in someone or something.

   b. one in which confidence is placed.

2. dependence on something future or contingent: HOPE

3. care, custody

4. in care of or possession of a trustee.

Wow! So based on the definitions' standpoint, faith, which is equivalent to trust, is to express complete confidence and reliance in or on one another; in this case **God**, strictly and solely on His character and ability to carry out any and all transactions on behalf of the trustee, **you and I**, without question or doubt as to His decisions and abilities.

Nowhere in this definition does it state or include the agreement or favorable, desired outcome of a person to whom the trustee is presiding over.

What exactly does this mean?

Well, in layman's terms, it means that regardless of the circumstance or position I find myself in, whether past, present, or future, I trust or have faith that the benefactor is working strictly on my behalf.

Now, the question remains clear, when we as Christians make the claim that we are believers or have faith, how does it play out when put it to the test?

Undoubtedly, I have found myself in various circumstances to which I believe God is at the forefront fighting on my behalf. There are, without question, a number of situations and experiences that I go through with an unshakable assurance that God is on my side, working on my behalf.

However, I have come across some instances where I've wondered if God was *'sleeping on the job'* or still with me due to the enormity or incredulity of what I was facing.

Now don't get me wrong. I don't want to dismiss the argument that the viewpoint of pressure remains and relies strictly on the person experiencing the dilemma, pain, or strife. This is most vital when understanding that what I may find challenging, you may find effortless; and what I may deem tolerant, you may feel unendurable.

These differences are only crucial to the understanding that each person focuses on individual challenges based upon their personal experiences and level of faith. It's important to keep in mind that unto every person is given a Measure of Faith.

When you think of **Faith**, I wonder what comes to mind?

Is it something that you have or something to be acquired?

Is it attached to being religious or Godly?

Is faith for everyone?

Is it ascribed to sinners and saints alike, or is it exclusive?

Is faith only for the Christian or can atheists possess it as well?

How necessary is it to have faith and be a Christian?

What measure of faith do I need to please God?

Can I mix faith and uncertainty and still be a believer?

Maybe you've contemplated the notion of faith but haven't really thought it through. Perhaps one or more of these questions have crossed your mind at some point in time? Or might it be possible that you have other questions, feelings and thoughts surrounding the concept of faith that you haven't thoroughly worked through yet. Either way, I would like to address my stance on faith, since the Lord has dealt with me.

Since salvation, until shortly before writing this book, I had almost always found myself asking for a greater measure of faith than the one I possessed because I felt as though I didn't have enough; or, that what I did have, was insufficient for the challenges and experiences I often found myself confronted with.

I was convinced that if I had more faith, I would stand strong long enough to not give in to my feelings of failure or yield my will to doubt. Nonetheless, no matter how much I prayed and sought after the Father with pleas of increasing my faith, He refused to hear my cry.

Over time, the difficulties, hardships, and trials that I faced would continue to always get the best of me, and what would once present itself as an opportunity to draw closer to the Lord, appeared to be the very thing separating me from Him.

Has that ever happened to you?

You pray for one thing and receive what seems to be the opposite?

You pray for patience and face contrariness.

You pray for peace and encounter turmoil.

You pray for temperance and struggle with voracity.

You pray for faith and are overwhelmed with uncertainties.

Today I want to encourage you. Today you've received just what you've asked for, the attainment of faith!

No, there is no secret formula or "magic" spell that I can share with you that will increase the volume of your faith, but instead what I will do is impart truth that will drastically change the way in which you view or see your faith.

The Father has shared some revelatory knowledge (that was readily available) regarding faith that, if received, will help your faith grow exponentially.

Ready?

"God hath dealt to each man a measure of faith." (Romans 12:3 ASV)

Yep! That's the revelation! Profound, isn't it?

I suppose you might receive this revelation in a different way if it wasn't something you already knew or heard, but that's what makes it so phenomenal. It was right there, in print, in front of us, available to access at any time.

Well, how does this make how you perceive faith any different?

I surmise that realizing you have something you thought you didn't might change the way you view YOUR faith.

You see, I believe that God has distributed faith equally among us, for *He is no respecter of persons.* (Romans 2:11)

In fact, we house the same measure of faith Jesus possessed!

Now I know you're thinking that what I am saying is ludicrous, but I believe that this is what Christ came to show us. Hebrews 11:6 states, *"For he that cometh to God must believe that He is, and that He is a rewarder of them that diligently seek Him,"* and it is utterly impossible for God to require of us something He did not already provide.

Shall I have the audacity to share with you that EVERYTHING we do and believe in is an expression of our faith?

Everything, and I mean everything requires faith. As a matter of fact, it takes just as much faith to believe as it does not to believe. It doesn't seem right. Yet, it is.

It takes faith to believe that Jesus was born of a virgin.

It takes faith to believe that Jesus died for our sin.

It takes faith to believe that we are forgiven.

It takes faith to believe that He saved us from death.

It takes faith to believe that He rose again on the third day and is seated at the right hand of the Father.

And perhaps that may not be simple enough for you to grab hold of.

The fact is that it already lies within you.

It takes faith to believe that He can maintain the sun in the sky.

It takes faith to believe that He formed the world in six days.

It takes faith to believe that He's coming back again.

But those are biblical truths, not necessarily faith in action.

It takes faith to believe that you'll wake up in the morning.

It takes faith to believe that you'll get to work safely.

It takes faith to believe that the cars will stay within the lines on the highway.

It takes faith to believe that you'll be paid at the end of the work week.

You see, it takes faith to do anything and everything that we do, so having faith is NOT the problem. The problem is adjusting how we distribute that faith. There are two kinds of faith that all people (Christians and non-Christians) alike operate in, optimistic and pessimistic.

Now, there's the optimistic Christian, or person who is hopeful and confident; and then there's the pessimistic Christian, or person whose mindset isn't very positive and doesn't have the belief that things will turn out right or in their favor. To be pessimistic means you believe evil outweighs the good and that bad things are more likely to happen.

This kind of thinking nullifies why Christ came and died for our sin and therefore it wouldn't make sense to ask for more faith so that you can further use it to believe a lie. But perhaps just knowing this doesn't ignite your faith the way you hoped it would. There's still hope.

When the man whose son was possessed with a spirit of torment approached Jesus and asked if *"*He can do anything, have compassion, and help us". And Jesus replied, "*Everything is possible for one who believes,*" and the boy's father responded, "I do believe; help me overcome my unbelief!" (Matthew 17:21-23)

Nowhere in the Bible does anyone ask for more faith, but instead to help unbelief.

That is the real problem. When we don't believe, we are actually telling God that we don't trust Him. It is impossible for faith and unbelief to exist at the same time. One must overcome the other.

As Christians we need to understand that faith is NOT a feeling. And sometimes we must disconnect from our emotions in order to align what we are thinking with the word of God. When we are experiencing difficulties and tests that come to challenge the faith that is within us, we need to stop, get in a quiet place, and seek God's consolation and comfort; and this only comes through having a relationship with Him. You cannot trust someone you don't know. And, most often, anyone who operates in unbelief is operating in fear. *"But God has not given us the spirit of fear; but of power, and of love, and of a sound mind."* (2 Timothy 1:7)

Jesus also states in Matthew 17:20, *"Truly I tell you, if you have faith as small as a mustard seed, you can say to this mountain, 'Move from here to there,' and it will move."*

Because it's not in the size of your faith, but rather how you use what you already have.

God is not a God of situation or of circumstance. He is God because He is God.

Situations and circumstances or hardships will arise in your life, not to test God but rather you and where you are in Him. You see, He is unchanging in His declaration and love and promises, but we are like the chaff in the wind (Psalms 1:4), unstable, easily swayed, and fickle, basing the ability of our God on our occasion rather than His reputation. Each of us, in our own way, lacks a full measure of faith, but not because it wasn't given or distributed evenly.

But rather because we have chosen to disperse it unequally, giving heed to thoughts, seducing spirits and ideologies that are not conducive to the God that we serve.

Therefore, let us strive to know Him, I mean really know Him, His nature, His truth, His love.

Being "broken" does not give us the liberty or right to deduce God to mere man as many of us often do in order to rationalize and justify our circumstances.

"Unto whom shall ye liken Me?" (Isaiah 40:18) In other words, whom will you compare God to?

Shall we take natural circumstances and hardships and those who have imposed them onto us and say that God is like them?

As a young girl, I grew up without a father and an extremely tough mother. Yes, she loved me, but she was also extremely critical of me and so more often than not, I felt insufficient and lacking as though there was nothing that I could do right in her eyes no matter how hard I tried. She loved me, but I rarely felt it although over time I've come to understand that this too, directly tied to her upbringing and childhood experiences. I had unknowingly become a part of a generational cycle of dysfunction that the enemy intended to use for my destruction if it was not recognized and stopped..

When I grew into a woman, I carried that same burden and philosophy over to God. I had been rejected throughout my life, so when I came to salvation, I imposed a critical mindset against myself and equated it to God's rejection of me.

He had never pushed me away. He had never forsaken me, and yet I was comparing Him to my upbringing and the constant disappointment I felt I was.

Later in life, as I continued to face other struggles, I equated those to my insufficiency and belief that I was being punished for not being good enough. He had never told me as much, but it was a truth I had experienced in the natural and therefore I translated everything through the eyes of disappointment and pain.

But this was not my lot. God wanted more for me, but I would have to trust that He wanted it for me. I had to muster up the courage to believe that the God who saved me and loved me, wanted to see me prosper, be happy and have peace. Mustering up this courage would take stirring up the faith that was already within me. I had to learn to redistribute my truths as I based them on the word of God and not my experiences.

He does this as part of the healing process not only for you but for others as well. Who will decide to walk that way so that you can show them how you were able to get through it and make your way back from the dark, with only the memory of that path leading you back.

But purposely, for those who watched you veer off the path knowing, expecting you would never find your way back, yet refusing to help you, or warn you, because of their jealousy and evil intention against you. No worries about them.

Assuredly they will get their reward, but not one second before they see, with their own eyes, how you emerge from the path looking stronger, walking straighter and closer to the finish line, with a bouquet of flowers in your hand for the next person you meet, without a singe of injury or hint of pain or setback, and they'll wonder for a second, "How'd you get over?"

But within the same breath you'll realize, *surely God was on that path with me ...*

Trusting in God

Lord, You are good, and Your mercy endures forever.

You alone are worthy of the praise, You alone are worthy of the glory.

Lord, help me trust You with my life. Help me to remember that You love me and that Your desire toward me is to give me a hope and a future.

You said that above all things that I should prosper and be of good health, even as my soul prospers. Prosper my soul, Lord.

Bless and keep all of the children that are in my care, that You have assigned for me to parent.

Teach me how to raise them in Your will and in Your ways.

When they confront trouble and difficult times, help me to remember that You love them more than I do and that You want to give them a hope and a future. That their lives are hidden in God through Christ Jesus.

Help me Father to pray without ceasing and to know that You have it all in Your hands.

Save my family and those who don't know You. Let my life be a living epistle.

Let my conversation align with what You say about me.

Father, you know me, you see the condition of my heart.

Give ear to my prayer, O God, and hide not thyself from my supplication.

I am asking for your divine grace and mercy.

I am, Abba.

Save my children, restore my family, cleanse my heart from all unrighteousness.

Give me unshakable, unmovable faith that can withstand the difficult times.

Uphold me with your love and sustain me with Your hand in every circumstance by Your unspeakable peace.

What seems impossible for man is possible for You Lord; therefore, let me lay all of my concerns at Your feet, knowing that You care for me and are working all things together for my good. seeking Your help.

You are a very present help in times of trouble, which means that You are always with me, especially in difficult times.

Help me to put my confidence in You and remember that all things are working together for my good because I love You and I am called for Your purpose.

In Jesus' name I pray.

Amen.

Chapter 3: What Do You Do When Faith Dies?

There is an emptiness so great that no substance can fill, where enjoyment can no longer be found, and brokenness prevails. It derives from the void of faith. Its absence creates an indescribable ache that runs through the current of one's veins, penetrating the heart until it bleeds anguish and hopelessness, diminishing life and causing every cell in your body and mind to scream from the agonizing feeling of defeat.

It causes an inexplicable pain that resists rationale and reasoning and robs the very peace from your mind as you witness it open-eyed yet feeling unable to stop it.

When faith falters, you find yourself in a lonely dark place in which prayers seem to go unanswered and God seems far too busy to stop by and see about you.

One day, feeling broken and frustrated, I asked God to give me a lobotomy. I was in desperate need of a brain transplant because I felt as if I could no longer survive with the memories of my past failures overtaking my mind, so much so that there was no room for life, happiness, or peace. I had no resolve. I begged and reasoned with God to remove the hellish thoughts that flowed through my head like poisonous toxins – toxins which inhibited me from thriving.

It was like having cancer and taking chemotherapy with a collapsed vein.

I wanted the cure, even attempted to find a solution in a desperate gasp at survival, and yet there seemed to be not one receiving signal at the other end of the line.

How could I operate and function as a Christian if I was tormented with bondage from within?

I felt locked off, suffocated by self-condemnation, and overcome with feelings of unworthiness, shame, guilt, and unacceptance. In the face of rejection, life can almost become hopeless, and betrayal can make you leery of every kind word and true intention.

Without faith, you begin to build walls that not only block people and God out of your life, but unbeknowingly lock you into a place of isolation and vulnerability to the enemy as well. In Christ there should be no such walls. If God is a healer, a restorer, a deliverer, and a comforter, why can't we dispel every negative thought with a simple snap? Why can't the act of simply accepting salvation be enough to change the way we think?

What happens to the level of your faith, if as a Christian you no longer believe God is on your side? How is it possible to make progress?

What happens when the evils and injustices of this life strangle your faith to death?

A husband leaving; a child passing away; the abandonment of a parent; the loss of a home or job; false accusations; being misunderstood and misjudged; the feeling as if no one could or will ever love you?

How do you respond to the idea that anything within your possession or desire can be stripped or denied you at any given moment for no apparent reason?

I say all this not to glorify the lack of faith, but more importantly to give it a face and a feeling.

To be able to picture it in a substantial, tangible way that can be so real, and yet so overwhelming that it snatches your breath and stifles your life to the point where life may even seem impossible.

We must be willing to acknowledge that regardless of the circumstances we encounter, anytime we talk negatively we are secretly implying, "God, is not enough," and that is the ultimate expression of faithlessness.

"For he that comes to God must believe that He is, and that He is a rewarder to them that diligently seek Him." (Hebrews 11:16)

God hates unbelief because it places emphasis on our fallen humanity which causes us to forget God's deity in it all. And therefore rather than looking at God's grace (which is sufficient for us) in spite of our shortcomings, which is what specifically makes Him God to us, we place our focus on where we've fallen short as though He is unable to redeem us because of our sin.

We must remind ourselves: I am who God says I am. God's validation IS enough. It has nothing to do with my belief in myself or my ability to succeed, where I come from, how I process my experiences, or who I understand myself to be. It definitely isn't who people say I am, acknowledge or don't acknowledge me to be, because they may never think anything of me. I may never even be worthy of a thought in their mind. Instead, it has everything to do with God and my belief and recognition that He is who He says He is and even more than who I could ever believe Him to be.

His validation says, "I think you're enough," or better yet, "I know that what I've placed in you IS ALL you need (to get you from here to there)."

If I limit God, it doesn't make Him limited, but it does limit my ability to see Him as He is.

1 John 3:2 says, *"Beloved, now we are the sons of God, and it doth not yet appear what we shall be; but we know that, when He shall appear, we shall be like Him; for we shall see Him as He is."*

Hebrews 11:1-6 reads, *"Now faith is the substance of things hoped for, the evidence of things not seen. For by it the elders obtained a good report. Through faith we understand that the worlds were framed by the word of God, so that things which are seen were not made of things which do appear."*

"By faith, Abel offered unto God a more excellent sacrifice than Cain, by which he obtained witness that he was righteous, God testifying of his gifts: and by it he being dead, yet speaketh."

By faith Enoch was translated that he should not see death; and was not found, because God had translated him: for before his translation he had this testimony, that he pleased God. But without faith it is impossible to please him: *"For he that cometh to God must believe that He is ..."*

... That He is what?

That He is God!

Ephesians 3:20 states, *"Now unto him that is able to do exceeding abundantly above all that we ask or think, according to the power that worketh in us."*

And what is that is power that working in us?

FAITH! Exceedingly and abundantly!

In other words, now unto Him who is able to do abundantly (in large quantities; plentifully), and not only in large quantities, not just enough, but surpassing enough and even more than that!

More than you ask for…

More than you can think about…

More than you pray for…

More than you can imagine…

More than you can do in your own strength…

But it's based in accordance with the level that you are willing to exercise your faith. In other words, you're only going to see the manifestation of who He is in conjunction to who you think He is to you.

He's a healer, but He can't be that to you if you don't believe.

He's a way maker, deliverer, miracle worker, promise keeper … but if you don't think He is, then He can't be that to you.

In Matthew 17:20, Jesus said, *"Because you have so little **faith**. Truly I tell you, if you have **faith** like a grain* *of **mustard seed**, you can say to this mountain, 'Move from here to there,' and it will move. Nothing will be impossible for you."*

It may be hard to believe this, but everything that you've gone through was necessary to get you to the destination God had for you. Though our choices may be the center cause of our own affliction, God's mercy and love is perfected so well beyond our faults that He uses our mistakes to shape us into His perfected image of us.

When you depend on God, it is His strength that works for you. When you depend on yourself, you are carrying your own weight, in your own strength, and eventually you will grow weary and faint.

But everything that you've been through has a purpose for power to impact someone else's life. Through your experiences and your trials, you will be challenged by God because he knows what the ultimate outcome of your testimony will be both for yourself and to others.

Everyone has been given a measure of faith. We choose whether or not to believe.

Jesus said, "*If you believe not...you are already condemned.*"

Peter demonstrated faith over fear by yielding to the Master's word when he asked, "If that be you Lord bid me to come." "And Jesus simply replied, "Come."

Know that if He's sending you to do a thing, He has already equipped you to do it and succeed because we are not operating from a position of seeking to obtain victory; we are operating from a position of already having the victory.

However the scripture denotes that sometimes we *"pray amiss"*, but and this because we have not sought God's intention and purpose for our lives (especially in a particular season), but instead we commonly pray for what we desire the outcome to be, rather than to have His purpose to be fulfilled.

We must remember, He knows the ending of a thing before its beginning therefore God is NEVER wasting the time He's vested in us because He knows the outcome of our life before we've taken our first breath!

The Bible states that at the 4th watch of the night (this is between the hours of 3 a.m. and 6 a.m.) Jesus came walking on the water towards the ship, and they were all fearful, nevertheless Peter must have felt something in his spirit that led him to call out to Jesus and ask Him if it indeed was Him, could he bid him to come.

Job 9:8 and Psalms 77 tells us that, "*God treads on water*," therefore it seems as though Jesus was demonstrating His deity, and Peter had enough faith and understanding of who Jesus was that he trusted Him to keep him if He stepped out of the boat at his bidding. However, when contrary winds arose they caused Peter to take His eyes off of the very thing he was trusting to sustain him.

We must recognize that, in this world, circumstances will arise from the enemy with the intention to cause you to forget about the deity of Christ and lose sight of what God has destined for you – if you take your eyes off Jesus.

We need to stay focused and call on Him, and rest assured that He will answer.

What Peter needed to recognize, and we need to learn from Peter, is that Peter was never able to walk on water in the first place, and that he wasn't fearful as much as he was doubtful.

Otherwise he would have questioned how could winds cause him to lose the ability to do something that he was never able to do without Christ in the first place?

In this Christian walk, we need to understand that we must truly learn to recognize and overcome doubt more than fear.

The Bible states, *"If you believe in your heart and doubt not..."* Mark 11:23

"A double minded man is unstable in all his ways..." James 1:8

"All things are possible to them that believe..." Mark 9:23

Everything that we need is not in Him, it IS Him.

Deception and planting seeds of doubt was Satan's plan from the very beginning. God said I created them – meaning Adam and Eve – in my image, and yet the enemy was able to plant the idea that if they ate of the tree of good and evil they would be as gods, therefore they ate the fruit, not recognizing that they were already created in His image.

Doubt has a way of tainting the knowledge and information that God has already given us. In Adam and Eve's case, doubt caused them not only to second guess who they were, but it also manifested itself when they wanted to take control of their own lives apart from God.

This error caused them to fall into sin because they sought after something they could not recognize they already possessed.

Doubt is a faith killer because it will always cause you to call into question God's voice and unsteady your step and ability to trust in Him when things become difficult. Doubt will also cause you to stay contrary when you think there should be peace.

So, what can you do when faith dies?

You can bury it, or you can give it water which is representative of the Spirit of God; and then you wait for the Son to shine upon those seeds with the light of His understanding until they begin to grow again.

Remember, He which has begun a good work in you is able to perform it, (Philippians 1:6) and God will NEVER leave you or forsake you. (Hebrews 13:5)

I Shall Not Want

Father, I come to You in the precious name of Your son Jesus Christ, giving thanks and Praise, for You are good and Your mercy endures forever.

Father, I thank You because there is no lack in You.

Lord, You supply my every need and I shall not want.

Father, I thank You because You are mindful of me.

You place the right people in my pathway.

You lead me and guide me into all truth.

You comfort me when I am weary and weak minded.

When I feel lonely, You show me that You are near.

When I am hungry You feed me, not only natural food for my nourishment, but spiritual food for my strengthening and understanding where I lack thereof.

Your kindness extends far beyond my reach and Your grace is above my comprehension.

When I am weak, there You are strong.

Where I lack faith, there You reveal Yourself as the one true God, able and willing to supply all of my needs according to Your riches in glory.

How great and mighty are You Father.

Creator of heaven and earth, giver of life, extension of love, provider, prosperer, fulfilled, motivator, encourager, healer, redeemer, deliverer, salvation.

There is none before You, none after You, none like You.

My one true shepherd who cares for me like no other.

The Lord is my keeper and I shall not want for any good thing, for it is Your good pleasure, to even give me the kingdom if I ask You and it brings glory to Your name.

Help me to remember this, that I pray not amidst or when I ask for things that You withhold from me for my good, for the sake of Your edification.

For I am Yours, bought with a price that I could not pay.

I am the apple of Your eye and the workmanship of Your hands.

You love me and vow to withhold nothing from me for Your namesake.

Oh, how I love You Father, because Your love is immeasurable and beyond understanding.

Help me to walk according to Your laws and precepts that You may be edified through my life.

Use me for Your honor for You said that if You be lifted up, You would draw all men to Yourself, for You wish that none should perish, but all should come to repentance.

I want for nothing when I recognize that You have me safely in Your arms, under Your wings and are continuously preparing a table before me in the presence of my enemies.

Surely goodness and mercy shall follow me all the days of my life and I will dwell in the house of the Lord forever.

I don't need anything because in You I have everything.

In Jesus' name I thank You for an extension of love I ever asked for and received, although I didn't deserve it, yet You who were counted worthy, found me worthy.

What a mighty God we serve!!!

Father, help my unbelief that my faith may flourish in the water of your Presence.

In Jesus' name I pray.

Amen.

Chapter 4: The Clock Is Ticking

One day, many years ago, I was awakened in the wee hours of the morning with an impending urgency from God to respond. I was tired but understood that something was bothering me at that very moment, and yet I still felt hesitant to move, get up or act. My thoughts were to stay in bed and sleep, but the Spirit said, "NO, NOW, GET UP, GO, MOVE!"

How often does the Spirit of God prompt us to move and respond to His call, His urgency and yet we procrastinate, are lazy, or not necessarily in tune with the move of God. We take Him for granted, ignore His beckoning, and put off for an unpromised tomorrow the things we can and should do today.

We need to recognize that our time on this earth, whether wasted or well spent, has the ability to reveal the ugliest truth or the utmost beauty about what lies beneath the surface of our belief in God.

What has your time thus far revealed to you about yourself?

We must recognize that we will never find time to do anything for God worthwhile if we remain dormant. If we WANT time, WE must make a conscious effort to find it. We cannot rely on our feelings because they will deceive us. If we choose to wait until the time is right to pray, trust, or seek God, we'll always find ourselves waiting because it never will seem to be the right time. We need to know that until we value ourselves and who God created us to be, we won't value our time. And until we choose to value our time, we will not do anything of value with it. If we want to make good use of our time, we've got to know how to recognize what's most important and then give it our all.

What may present itself as free time or careless distractions can in fact be extremely expensive! Everything costs time and attention; and the reality is, nothing in life is free. Even salvation cost something, even though it was extended to us for free, it was paid for with a hefty price.

We also have to understand that time is not a renewable resource and once it's gone, there is no recouping it; therefore we have to spend our time wisely on things that matter. So, if you and I are going to invest our time in anything, let us invest it in what we believe is valuable and we will end up with a treasure trove of what we took the time to collect. Wasting time on what we *believe* is valuable (at the time), that in fact isn't, will leave us with nothing to show for it except regret and unfinished business.

It is important to acknowledge that our time here on earth is but a vapor, and we must maximize it to its fullest. Only what we do for God is going to last, so let us lay a strong foundation upon which to build.

This doesn't mean that we will be free from distractions and difficulties. In fact, the enemy will assuredly bring about a variety of trouble and nonsensical things to consume our time, and if we are not careful, so much of it can be wasted focusing on the wrong things.

Occasionally, there are moments in time where it can appear as though some lessons in life that were specifically designed to strengthen and build our faith were mishandled, misunderstood, and taken for granted or disregarded for its intended purpose, and God, in His perfection, grants us more grace to accomplish what He desired the outcome to become, while more time elapses.

Sadly, what could have been accomplished on faith's timeline within days, weeks, or months, may become deferred by one year, or many, many years. Eventually, one may fall so far behind schedule because of their lack of understanding God's plan for our lives that in order to catch us up and shorten the gap, one may experience a season of intentional victories and moments that only speak of God, His sovereignty, His power, and His love designed to purposely catch us up to where we were supposed to be in God's timeline.

And during that course of time, we become acutely aware of who God is, and what He's purposely doing as a means of divulging His omnipotence, omnipresence, and omniscience; truth be told, our finite, fleshly minds could never truly understand the vast extent to which the truth of God's power extends. Nonetheless, it is God's intended purpose to hasten our current understanding for us to make progress in Him.

Then, suddenly for what appeas to seem like no "apparent" reason, we come to a standstill, an empty, wilderness-type place where everything that has been poured into us is being tested and tried in the fire for resilience and purification.

It is a time to see if what we have attained can withstand in the face of adversity…and if it does, and remains we will have steadily made forward movement in successfully increasing our faith, and then we will reach another level in God where new challenges begin based on our new standing in God.

However, if, when that deposit, in the face of adversity, shakes and proves itself to be unstable, the opposite happens. It becomes wasted away as the chaff carved by the wind, dwindling until once again you are stymied at the base level, needing to begin again. Like the circling of the mountain, this process can be time consuming and painstakingly slow in progress.

But this morning God told me that a 911 signal had been sent out. That time is of the essence and no longer available for lollygagging. There is an urgency in the spirit that is saying time has almost run out.

So, what exactly does that mean?

The end of the world?

Is Jesus coming?

No. I mean, yes He's coming, but that's not the urgency God is speaking of. From the moment you and I got saved, and all the time before that, until now, He has been preparing us for specific events that will come one day to challenge every principle we have been taught to believe in and the knowledge we have acquired through our encounters with the Father.

They are tests to reveal the substance that lies within us and the source of our strength, and that outcome will determine our future progress as a witnesses and children of God. Some of us will excel and move forward to the next level in God to do bigger and greater things, while others will come up short, lacking, or emptyhanded, and be required to take the test again before progressing.

That urgency, the spirit voiced to me, is the warning signal for an impending test that is coming to challenge the very fiber of the foundation upon which you and I stand. It was prepared for us before we were formed in our mother's belly and tweaked and perfected throughout our life based upon how we think and what we believe. It was set up by the enemy to be our undoing yet orchestrated by God to place a trophy in our hands.

You see, we will be required to pull out every resource that has been provided to us through the word and the experiences we've had.

We will be required to remember the days when we "walked" on water, called down fire, heard the abundance of rain, were fed by ravens, thrown in the lion's den, thrown in the furnace, faced the giant, marched around Jericho, lived in the king's palace, locked in prison, or faced the Red Sea with the Egyptians closing in. It's only through these experiences that we see who God is, and for no reason other than believing, and holding on to God's unchanging hand and promises.

So, what exactly does this have to do with time?

We must be cognizant of how we use it from the moment we wake up and open our eyes to the time we close them to go to sleep. We cannot continue to waste it when we live in a dying world that's waiting for us to take our positions and answer our call. *"For the creation waits in eager expectation for the children of God to be revealed."* Romans 8:19

We must not get caught up in distractions, or sidetracked to the point where we are so misaligned from our destiny, that we miss our calling altogether.

So, now that we've established that yesterday's gone, and tomorrow's unknown, what do we do with today?

Time is of the essence! We need to learn how to value each moment as it is given. "How do we do that," you might ask. Well, we do it by making a transition – which simply means – it's time to change and glorify our Father with purpose and intention.

Lord, Help Me Let Patience Have Her Perfect Work

Father, in the name of Jesus, I come to You now giving You thanks, praise, and glory.

There is none like You.

I honor You for who You are and how You do!

Lord, I'm asking today that You teach me how to let patience have her perfect work in my life. Yes, I know that I will be tried by fire so that I may be refined like gold, but I ask that You help me to be patient with the process.

That during these trying times that I let patience have her perfect work and not seek to understand what You are doing, but instead to embrace it.

Father, I know that most times I kick against the pricks and try to circumvent the pain in the moment, which has a far more exceeding weight in glory.

Every trial and situation are designed to be for my good, even those things that are meant to destroy me.

So in the name of Jesus, I ask that You remind me when I'm going through difficult times or that the burdens seem too much to bear, not to stop pressing in, because You are trying to establish me and secure my footing.

That after doing all to stand, I stand in the profession of my faith with the assurance that it is all working for my good and solidifying my faith in You.

Help me to trust in You with my whole heart and mind and soul and lean not to my own understanding but in all my ways acknowledge You and You will direct my path even when it takes me directly through the fire, because You are using moments like those to bring me into the full truth of who I am and what I am able to accomplish in You.

Don't let me faint in times of adversity, but instead help me to put on the whole armor of the Lord, and to be strong in You and the power of your resurrection.

Lord, complete the work which You have begun in me and see it to completion so that I can prove what is the perfect will of God.

These things I ask in Jesus' precious name.

Amen.

Chapter 5: Trust in God, Don't Fall Back on Cliches and Idioms

There are common cliches that say things like: anything that can go wrong, will go wrong, and usually does; it's easier said than done; what goes up, must come down; a bird in the hand, beats two in the bush; it's hard to kick against the pricks; if it weren't for bad luck, I wouldn't have any luck at all.

Such statements and formulations of thinking, deceptively ease us into accepting whatever life brings our way. It's almost like slipping into a warm bath – it just feels comfortable. Think about it: it's almost easier to believe in nothing than to hope for anything, isn't it?

The latter of the two makes us vulnerable and subject to the possibility of disappointment and failure, while the former accepts calamity as the norm, while discrediting a blessing as a mishap or an unexpected surprise.

Why should we trouble our trouble with the rhapsodic hope of something greater than our present circumstance?

Isn't it better to leave well enough alone?

Why not confer with the scripture that says things like, *"You have not because you ask not."* (James 4:2) *It is the Father's good pleasure to give you the kingdom.* (Luke 12:32)

"He who did not spare His only son but gave Him up for us all, how will He not also give us all things." (Romans 8:32)

Or better yet, *"The steps of a good man are ordered by the Lord,"* (Psalms 37:23) and *"I know the plans I have for you, declares the Lord; plans to prosper you and not to harm you, plans to give you a hope and a future."* (Jeremiah 29:11)

And while these promises do not guarantee we will never face adversity, they should at least reassure us that God has everything under His control and ultimately, all things will work together for our good, because God loves us and we are called according to his purpose. Romans 8:28

However, in order for God's word to be successfully activated and accomplished in our lives, we must first conceive it within our spirits. We must hope beyond what our eyes can see, venture beyond what our hands can touch, imagine beyond what our minds can think, savor beyond what our lips can taste, listen beyond what our ears can hear, perceive beyond what our nose can smell, and trust beyond what our hearts can bear.

Our perception on what we see, based on what we feel or where we're going, are often confused because we allow our natural senses of seeing and hearing and experiencing to ignite a sense of doubt. When we experience realities outside our spiritual expectation, we can sometimes have predisposed responses which are rooted in strongholds and familiar spirits.

There are open doors to doubt. Sometimes we require a physical response, or proof that God is not willing to give. Things enter our soul through our heart. Often, we don't feel faith-filled, and you can't convince yourself to believe in something you don't believe in.

These unabashed efforts push us toward and facilitate the notion that we must propel beyond our own simplistic understanding, subject to flaws, and rely on faith.

And what is faith?

Belief in God!

Not based on proof or substantiated by fact, but rather confidence and trust without reasonable doubt, that despite how things may appear or feel, God has the upper hand in our lives and His Will shall prevail.

Nevertheless, we will be tried, and challenges will arise. And the question becomes a matter of: not if adversity comes, but rather when adversity comes, what will we do?

Shall we concede defeat?

Should we relinquish the promise?

Shall we surrender the hope and allow whatever will be to be?

"But we are not those who draw back and are destroyed, but we are those who have faith and obtain life." (Hebrews 10:39)

"The Kingdom of Heaven suffered violence and the violent take it by force." (Matthew 11:12)

And what exactly does this mean to the Christian today?

It simply means despite whatever may come against us, we will not surrender our position in Christ and allow the enemy to steal the knowledge of who we are in Him and distort our belief, but rather we will contend against the devourer, through faith trusting that *"He which has begun a good work in us is able to perform it."* (Philippians 1:6)

"For God is not a man that he should lie, nor the son of man that he should repent. Has he said it, and will he not do it? Or has he spoken, and will he not make good?" (Numbers 23:19)

Therefore, by confession, and sometimes action, we need to continue to press forward against all odds. So let us see further than the eye can see and not think it better to be safe than sorry, but rather be like them who also knew God (to be strong) and do great exploits. (Daniel 11:32)

We will not expect the normal or conduct business as usual. But our norm instead will be daring to be different, and our usual will become trusting in God.

So why is it then that during our walk with Christ we come to junctures that appear to be just out of his reach?

Have you believed him for a new car or house, but that job seems impossible?

Have you believed him for salvation or deliverance but not healing from cancer?

Have you ever believed God for a loved one or your marriage, but it's too far-fetched for a barren woman to have a baby?

You see, within each of us lies that measure of faith and yet, despite its size, we alone with God are responsible for nurturing it, protecting it, and growing it.

What's in your mind's eye can make some things appear more possible than others?

How do we delegate what we feel God can and cannot, do?

Is it by our experiences, our situations, our circumstances, our faith?

If we can conceive it, does that make it possible; and if it seems too outlandish, does that make it impossible?

The scripture says, *"Now unto him that is able to do exceedingly and abundantly above all that we ask or think, according to the power that works in us."* (Ephesians 3:20) Therefore, if it is according to the power that worketh in us do we, with our thought, have the power to undo such great works?

Are our thoughts greater than God?

Jesus himself said, *"If thou can't believe all things are possible to him that believeth."* (Mark 9:23)

I've heard many times in the church realm, "Take the limit off God." What exactly is the limit that we speak of or impose on Him? It is the one that says God can do this, but He can't do that!

We must remember that: He can do all things but fail. We should live each precious moment that has been given to us to the fullest, maximizing His promises towards us because one day we will have to give an account of what we did with what God gave us; and faith in His word will be the measure by which we are gaged.

Clichés will serve no purpose other than causing us to fall into a monotony of untruths that seek to define God, who cannot be explained in the rationale of the human mind because He just IS; and what He says is true and apart from Him, and in that truth, we can do nothing without Him.

You're With Me, Even in the Lowest Valley

Father, in the name of Jesus Christ our Lord and Savior I come humbly before You today, thanking You for Your grace and mercy and peace in any and every circumstance.

Lord, I recognize that life happens, there is a season to everything under the sun.

We have good days and days when things don't quite go our way.

However, through it all, I've come to realize that all things are working together for our good.

Many times, we have circumstances that we find challenging and difficult,

times when we wonder if we've done something wrong, or if You've forgotten about us, but Your word says that You will never leave us alone or turn Your back on us…that is even true when we think we've failed You or know that we have done something wrong.

You are not in the position of abandoning Your children or bailing out when times get tough.

In fact, those are the times that You press in the most and make Yourself known as God.

When I find myself in the valley of despair, You are the God that feeds me, comforts me and lets those around me know that I am not alone.

You Father, offer a peace that passes all understanding including my own and that of others who may see me struggling openly.

Though my tank may seem empty, it's running over with Your goodness and grace that can sustain me.

All I need to do is trust and believe regardless of what I think or feel.

Remind me often that You are working behind the scenes that may be playing out before my eyes differently than I expected.

Help me to stay focused on Your promises, which never fails and gives me hope that Your desire for my future is a great one.

In this journey called life, we will face much adversity, nevertheless if we were to understand that most situations are to demonstrate the greatness of our God, rather than to accentuate our weaknesses or highlight our shortcomings.

And everything is for Your glory!

You implore us to be careful for nothing, but with prayer and supplication make our requests known unto You.

You are with me, even in the lowest valley.

Your compassion and love for me is immeasurable, and in the valley is where I can thrive and grow and flourish and blossom into the person who You have destined me to be before the beginning of time.

As the songwriter says, "If I never had a problem, I wouldn't know my God could solve them, I wouldn't know what faith in Your word can do.

To God be the glory, to God be the glory, to God be the glory for the things He has done."

I thank You Lord for considering me to show off how Majestic You truly are.

In Jesus' name I pray.

Amen.

Chapter 6: What You Don't Know Can Hurt You

Hosea 4:6 reads, *"My people are destroyed for a lack of knowledge."*

This scripture is synonymously used with the idea that we, people, Christians, fail to read our Bible daily, often or frequently enough in order for us to know God's word; and while that may ring true for most, I believe those words account for a far greater truth than we are willing to acknowledge or consider.

The dictionary defines knowledge as:

An acquaintance with facts, truths, or principles as from study or investigation, familiarity gained by site, experience or report something that is or may be known the body of truths or facts accumulated in the course of time.

It also defines lack as:

Deficiency or absence of something needed, desirable, or customary, something missing or needed.

So, while knowledge, in this scripture professes to be in possession of something, lack proves to be an absolute opposite, in that it is to be without possession of something.

Yet what is that something?

Is it information?

Is it enlightenment?

How about illumination or wisdom?

James 1:5 says, *"If any of you lack wisdom, let him ask of God, that give it to all men liberally, and upbraideth not, and it shall be given him."*

Believe it or not, what we lack as a people is not book smarts or comprehension, because God himself is able to provide these things and fill this gap.

In actuality, the rudimentary substance missing from this equation, is absolute or otherwise known as gospel truth.

The simple definition of truth is:

The real facts about something, a verified or undisputed fact, proposition or principle, conformity with fact or reality something that is known to be true.

Now, what I love about this particular definition, is that its rationale is based on evidence of true events or experiences resulting in the alteration of one's perception.

It happened; therefore it is conceived as reality.

However, what happens when the reality of a situation is not the truth?

Well, one might say, that's a contradiction! How can an indisputable fact not be true? Especially if it's based on what we know, because what exactly does "know" mean, since it is the root of the word knowledge?

To perceive or understand as fact or truth.

To apprehend clearly and with certainty.

To have established or fixed in the mind.

To be cognizant or aware of.

Therefore, if we have the facts, and we have the truth and the knowledge, of which we've seen, tasted or experienced, what exactly is missing from this equation? This is not what we should be asking ourselves.

The true question is not what don't we know, but rather who don't we know?

Daniel 11:32 reads, *"Those who do wickedly against the Covenant he shall corrupt with flattery, but the people who know their God shall be strong and carry out great exploits."*

Each of us at some point in our lives have experienced pain or suffering that somehow keeps us from moving forward. The fear of reliving, reviving, or repeating a past failure stagnates growth as we operate in a truth that we've been hurt, but not the truth that God is in control.

So, we must ask ourselves a pertinent question: who is God to me?

Is he fair?

Is he just?

Does he adhere to all of my requests, suggestions or requirements?

Is God my personal Genie at my disposal, there to Grant my every wish or command? Does he need my advice or prompting?

How well do we know God?

He is not concerned with our opinions or past experiences because they are not a basis for what He can and will do.

He is a deliverer.

He is a healer.

He is a way maker.

He is my all and all.

He is my provider, so what can I go through or experience in this life that can change that indisputable fact?

He does not conform because of a truth that you've come to know by way of a personal encounter. We cannot confine God within the small expansions of our mind.

Romans 11:34 reads, *"For who has known the mind of the Lord or who has been his counselor?"*

Isaiah 55:8 in the NLT reads, *"My thoughts are nothing like your thoughts, says the Lord, and my ways are far beyond anything you could imagine."*

Therefore, we can never base our future on our past, or look back into yesterday to see what tomorrow holds for us.

Inevitably if we do so we will be destroyed for our failure to progress.

This is what I believe to be the fundamental truth of God.

He loves us. We were created on purpose for a purpose. His Will will be done in my life regardless of any circumstance or experience – past, present, or to come.

And lastly, all things, whether good or bad, right or wrong are working out together for our good so that we may be complete, and whole, presented blameless before Him through Christ's sacrifice and to these facts there can be no contradiction.

And though reading it expressed this way and obtaining this knowledge may appear to be easy and obvious, the road by which it was obtained was nothing but. For in this life thus far, I have experienced hardships and trials, felt oppressed and depressed, with seemingly no real way out but to live it.

I've experienced divorce and abandonment, sickness and pain, heartache and disappointment, yet like the songwriter said:

*Through it all I've learned to trust in Jesus, and I've learned to trust in God, and I've learned to depend upon his word, (*not my thoughts).

*So, I thank God for the mountains, and I thank him for the valleys, I thank him for the many things he brought me through. For if I never had a problem, I wouldn't know my God could solve them, I wouldn't know what faith in his word can do. (*Andre Crouch)

And as I reflect over relationships and friendships forged, verified true, solidified faithful and then suddenly lost, I realize that unless God says it's forever, it probably isn't.

You see, as children of the most High, we can become easily distracted by the beauty of friendship or the familiarity of a job or the comfort of consistency to the point where we become lax, take things and God for granted, to the point where we are unwilling to let things go, see another way or believe God for new things.

Assuredly, while I'd love to be blessed and have new opportunities presented to me or receive unmerited favor through the association of new acquaintances or friends, I don't want to lose them to any connection or relationship I've come to hold so dear and true.

Why must God remove me from my comfort zone and disrupt my way of normalcy to bless me?

Why can't we have the new added on to what He's already established and settled in my life?

Simple. Because new wine cannot be poured into old vessels, lest they burst.

Each stage of Our Lives is a steppingstone into a new era and season of our lives and all stairways lead to God, but each level requires a new transition in order to get there.

Sometimes it may involve the removal of established friends and the addition of new ones; sometimes we may have to leave a familiar place or setting in order to find that *"city"* whose Builder and Maker is God.

And, while sometimes it requires an external transformation, it always requires an internal shift of our mindset.

Often, during the process of change, we experience more interruption through unforeseen opposition in the form of roadblocks utilized by the enemy as a way to slow us down or deter us from reaching our destiny.

But God, who is omnipotent, can strategically use a deterrent as a tool to build character and Faith within us. Hence, *"What was meant for evil God can turn around for my good."* (Genesis 50:20)

However, some oppositions are a flat out warning to keep us away to avoid a fall or an even worse fate. But we must learn to incline our ear to know which way the Lord wants to lead us.

Not everything we experience is meant for evil, while equally not everything is meant for our good.

Yet, if we are not in total acceptance of God's plan for our lives, it can make the removal or clean-up process that much more difficult for ourselves, not God!

The Bible says, he who loves his mother or father more than Me is not worthy of Me.

In other words, no circumstance, relationship, or desire should supersede God's purpose and plan for our lives. And if you find yourself in a struggle or kicking against the pricks, compromising or doing things that don't edify the kingdom, or if you find yourself feeling lost or destitute or broken, chances are you're not yielding to God's perfect will for your life.

Surely there are things in our life we want and need, valuable relationships or treasures we hold dear – even God himself wants us to be relational. And yet out there is a vat of blessings that promises a new beginning just waiting to overtake us and be poured out, but we are too full. We are full of ourselves, full of our past, full of our wants, and full of our old ways, and there is no room for the new until we've been emptied out!

Therefore, as we prepare our hearts and minds to transition, let the Lord guide us in reevaluating the inventory of Our Lives.

Are there things that we've been holding on to that it's time to let go of?

Do you have altars built to "other gods" in friendships, relationships, jobs, people, places?

Regardless of what it is, God has more and better if only we trust Him enough to submit to the changes that lie ahead knowing that, in the end, our ladder will be greater than our past.

Why Worry When We Can Pray?

Father, I come to You in the precious name of our Lord and Savior Jesus Christ boldly asking for mercy, grace, and peace.

Father, creator of heaven and earth, He who laid the foundation of the world before the beginning of time.

He who knows all things and created all things from the beginning to the end.

He who has no limit and holds all knowledge of yesterday, today, tomorrow, and forevermore.

Who, out of time, stepped into time so that You can make sense to me, the order of the days and weeks and months and years and decades to understand that nothing is impossible for You.

Father, you commanded that I should not worry or be anxious for anything, for all things are in Your hands.

You commanded that I commit my ways unto You, that I should pray and not faint.

That I should seek first the kingdom of God and all His righteousness, and by prayer and supplication, make my requests known unto You.

Is there anything too hard for You?

Are You not able to deliver today as You were yesterday?

What are my fears when You said that You did not give us the spirit of fear?

What are my concerns when You said that You know the plans that You have for me to give us a hope and a future?

Why should I worry when my steps are ordered by You Lord?

Are you not the same yesterday, today and forever?

Or is it possible that in my strife and anxiety I can sway the plan of God?

While You do love me, You are not moved by what I perceive.

I am engraved in the palm of Your hand.

I am Your workmanship and You are the Master craftsman.

Are You unable to make something glorious of my life if I put my trust in You?

You said He who spared His only son, would He not give us all things freely,

even the kingdom if we ask for it, if only we put our trust in You?

Father, remind me that in times of calamity and distress that You are near, even in my mouth, that Your desire is upon me and that You are willing and able to complete the work that You started in me.

So why should I? Am I worrying?

Do you not care for the birds, and they gather not, and the lilies and they toil not?

How much more then will You care for me and provide all that I need?

If You said it, I should believe it and that should settle it.

So Father I ask that You remind me that when I worry, it changes nothing, but when I pray You can and will change everything.

You take what the enemy meant for evil and You turn it for good, so why worry when I can pray?

I thank you Father for bringing to my remembrance how great and mighty and gracious and loving and kind You are. You will never leave me or forsake me and that my hope is in You.

I pray all these things in the precious name of Your only Son, Jesus Christ.

Amen.

Chapter 7: Are You Nearsighted, Farsighted or Blind?

"Now we see things imperfectly, like puzzling reflections in a mirror, but then we will see everything with perfect clarity." (1 Corinthians 13:12)

"The Lord seeth not as man seeth; for man looketh on the outward appearance, but the Lord looketh on the heart." (1 Samuel 16:7)

<u>Nearsighted</u>: When light enters (the cornea) and is refracted (sent) to the wrong place in the eye. This causes a person to be short sighted, giving them the ability to see objects clearly up close, but unable to focus on them further away.

<u>Farsighted</u>: Items far away are clear (but things like reading and knitting) become difficult because nearby objects appear fuzzy or unfocused.

<u>Astigmatism</u>: distorts objects both near and far, so that everything appears out of focus and shewed.

<u>Blind</u>: Unable to see, visually impaired; lacking perception, awareness, or discernment.

Seeing (parallel to knowing) who God is, is a process. When we are initially saved, we have that sense as if someone has just turned on the lights, as we begin to see things in a way we never have before, as if for the first time.

In a lovely transformative experience, we are able to see God in the now, and the great things He has wrought in the present. However, as we begin to cultivate our relationship with Him, we also begin to see how He was operating in our yesterday and become ever more hopeful for what tomorrow may bring. That clarity is as beautiful as seeing for the first time and having 20/20 vision.

Over time our sight can go through a distortion and become weakened by our disappointments, strained by unexpected outcomes and cloudy as though we suddenly have a filmy obstruction (like cataract) that is preventing us from seeing God as the faithful Father He is and has always been.

Like Thomas, who doubted Jesus, walked amongst them after His crucifixion, we may become nearsighted Christians, seeing Him only in the now, as circumstances and situations unfold in our favor or right before our eyes, as long as they aren't far-fetched or too unreasonable to believe.

To see things up close doesn't require us to have an exorbitant amount of faith when it relates to everyday scenarios to which we can almost predict the outcome or see them as they happen.

Some of us can only see God when He bids you to walk on the water and steadies your first few steps, after you've touched His nail printed hand and beheld His face, or in response to bringing your dead child to life. When you can only see God when He's close, you are a nearsighted Christian.

However, have you ever found yourself in the odd position of being able to see God in everyone's experience but your own?

Knowing (but truly not knowing) the nature and power of the God you serve can give one the unique ability to understand what *He Is able to do* for everyone in your pathway because you are able to see Him from afar, outside of your own circumstances. It may be perhaps linked to an experience where you once saw clearly, which gave you the foundation you needed to know God's nature enough to see His salvation, grace and ability to deliver others, yet somehow you can't believe the same faith applies to you.

This is how farsighted Christians operate. They see God's hand and power to save others but not necessarily themselves, because those circumstances are too close and are based more on personal experiences and circumstances.

As a believer, and I say this term facetiously, is it not difficult to look at an impossible situation someone (other than yourself) might be struggling with, and be able to see that God can pull them through?

At some point in my life, I too went from seeing things clearly in my life with God's divine mercy, to not being able to see at all. I often found myself encouraging others in varying situations that ranged from the possible to the improbable knowing the nature of the God I served.

I was gifted with words of encouragement on how to navigate faith through difficult and trying times as a way to strengthen others when their solution was unclear.

Ironically, I was not so astute at navigating the storms of my own tumultuous sea.

I secretly was a farsighted Christian, unable to see my way out of things clearly and how God was on my side working things out for my good, especially when the obstacles and difficulties were relatively close. I couldn't see the end from the beginning.

And when it came to my personal life, my children, and my family, some of those struggles were absolutely unbearable because they weren't supposed to happen to me. I was saved! How could I possibly find God in a situation that wasn't supposed to happen at all (as far as I was concerned)? As though God would spare me from heartache through my salvation.

And yet, the truth is, He absolutely could have saved me from the heartache, had I leaned into Him instead of my own understanding.

Heaven is the end goal, but the path to getting there is riddled (stained) by obstacles outside of our control.

Like Elijah, despite calling fire down from heaven and seeing it manifest, we find ourselves under a juniper tree waiting to die when Jezebel says, our fate is in her hands. This happened even when he knew who God was and had seen His power manifested in phenomenal ways.

Many times, as believers, we examine our lives through an obscure lens. Why?

Because it has been tainted by our skewed perceptions, opinions and ideologies based upon past or present experiences.

Grace through faith, is most usually omitted since we forget that God does not measure success or accomplishment on the same scale of judgment that we so often do.

And though experience has the potential to serve as life's best teacher of all natural things, it holds little credibility when predicting the pathway that God has designed for us.

When we're implored to *"lean not to our own understanding"* (Proverbs 3:5-6), God the Father is trying to make us aware that how we think is often related to how we feel, or where we find ourselves and is almost always not aligned with His thoughts about, or for us.

Believer, as Sons and Daughters of the most High God, we need to first understand that there is a difference between arrogance and confidence.

Arrogance, as spoken of in Romans 12:2-4, allows one person the audacity to think that he or she is better than the next. Arrogance says, "I was able to keep myself because who I am and what I possess is greater than what you do."

Confidence, however, is equated to knowing that despite the challenges we face, God is not only able, but *will work every circumstance to the benefit of our good* (Romans 8:28-30) because His mercy and Grace abounds in us towards our perfecting.

Secondly, we need to remember that there is no coincidence in God. We did not haphazardly stumble into God's love, and we didn't take a wrong turn and accidentally find God.

God carefully and purposely chose us, as explained in John 15:16.

And because there are no coincidences, and because we were handpicked, we can never surprise God by our actions, thoughts, feelings, or choices. In Isaiah 46:10, He says, *"Declaring the end from the beginning, and from ancient times, things which have not been done saying my purpose will be established."*

In Job 8:7, He states, *"Though your beginning was insignificant, yet your end will increase greatly."*

In Ecclesiastes 3:11, it states, *"He has made everything beautiful in his time; also He has set the world in their heart, so that no man can find out the work that God makes from the beginning to the end."*

Therefore, although we sometimes fail, we never fail God because He always knew the choices we would make and yet He chose us anyway.

It is only by the spirit that we are convicted because we desire to do better, and the enemy who antagonizes us to feel as though missing the mark somehow disqualifies us because God was not expecting ***that*** from us.

Let us therefore be watchful and having eyes in the spirit, see clearly the things which God has for us so that we may avoid the snares and pitfalls the enemy tries to use to dissuade, distract and deter us from our journey in Christ to God the Father.

To have astigmatism is to be confused and unable to focus on neither the things God had done nor the things that He is doing in one's life. This person toggles between faith and doubt so commonly that they are unable to trust past their personal perception. The bible says that such a person is considered a double-minded man and unstable in all his ways. (James 1:8)

But what exactly does it mean to be blind?

To be blind is not to see God at all.

That is to miss all of the beauty and wonder that surrounds us. To deny love and to negate favor is to say with disregard for Christ's sacrifice that you have been forgotten or forsaken.

Sometimes one can become **blinded** by the troubles of this life or lose sight of who He is and fail to recognize that God is still God no matter what we experience, no matter how dark the road or how much we may have lost our way.

We equate the apparent unfairness that lies within the world to the God of our salvation, but none of that speaks to God and who He is, was, has been and will always be. Jesus speaks of those who, having eyes, see not because they didn't understand, nor seek to know who God really was.

Let us therefore strive to retain our sight, even if we occasionally find ourselves groping through the darkness, maintain confidence that He is leading us safely to the other side of victory.

We have to be able to see it, so that we can declare it!

Vision has to be spoken first before it can be manifested in the physical.

Vision is the mind's eye to see beyond the natural.

Habakkuk's vision was talking about the return of Christ. Isaiah said, *"He declares the end of a thing at the beginning of it!"* and *"The glory of God shall be revealed, and ALL shall see it."* (Isaiah 46:10, 40:5)

Vision is the manifestation of God's glory. We must see the vision before we speak the vision, and we must speak the vision before we write the vision. Hope is something that isn't born, yet you are preparing for it. Vision is not out there in the atmosphere; vision lies within you and can never be manifested until it first is seen.

Hope sees what it sees from the inner you. Hope is earnest expectation standing with an outstretched neck and visionaries expect it even when they have yet to see it.

If you close your eyes and see nothing, that is probably why you see nothing with your eyes open. Hope takes on the form of an outstretched neck.

Hope sees it in the spirit realm first.

If you can envision it, it's just a matter of time before you give birth to it, this is why you have to say what you see until you see what you say! We're going to have to learn how to operate from the neck down, get out of our heads and get in the spirit. Change what you see because what you see is what you become pregnant with, and what you become pregnant with is the only thing you'll give birth to.

The first visionary was God Himself. He is able to see our shall be, despite where we currently find ourselves, which is the reason why he chose us in the first place.

Your focus is your vision! In other words, your steps will be directed by what you believe will manifest itself next. Remember the vision God has given you is not just for you. The moment you stop seeing, you hinder a generation; however, people can never receive from anyone they cannot see.

If we're going to see the full manifestation of God's purpose for earth, we're going to need to work the vision. True ministry is inclusive of everything God has imparted in our life.

If God gives us vision He didn't give the vision to us "just because". He wants us to know that this vision is our ministry; He gave it to us because we are responsible for cultivating those visions and bringing them into manifestation.

My Help

Father, Divine creator of heaven and earth.

Everything is Yours and all things belong to you.

You inspire gifts, You give health, You love unconditionally,

You give strength to the weak and courage to the timid.

Lord, You own the cattle on a thousand hills and everything that is seen was made by You, and nothing that is made was made without You.

Father,

If Your word be true, I can never want for any good thing.

Lord, You said that You supply All of my needs according to Your riches in glory.

You knew me before I was created in my mother's womb, You know the number of tears I've shed and have them bottled up in heaven.

Even the very hairs on my head are numbered by You.

What is man that Thou art mindful of him?

Who am I that You should love me?

And yet You do.

My help comes from the Lord everlasting.

The creator of heaven and earth, of the seen and unseen, my God lives in me.

You are a Very present help in the time of trouble.

Therefore Father, I come before You today asking for Your divine protection for me and my family.

You said no weapon formed against the righteous shall prosper, and we are Your righteous in Christ Jesus.

Bring the plans of the enemy to nought, stop the mouths of the gainsayers and those who wish me evil.

What was meant for my destruction, turn it around for my good.

And Father, I ask that You forgive me for any wrong thoughts or actions, for every sin which has so easily beguiled me.

And I ask that You create in me a clean heart and renew a right spirit within me.

Help me to trust in You with all my heart and my mind and my strength and lean not to my own understanding, but in all my ways acknowledge You so that You can get the glory from my life this day and forevermore.

Thank you, Father for being my help, for in my weakness Your strength is made perfect.

In Jesus' name, Amen.

Chapter 8: The Faithless Believer

When we refuse to hear God's voice, and we choose to go our own way without heeding His warning or directives, how can we possibly expect a positive outcome?

Our premise is to do the will of the Father, but how can we know His will, if we're not willing to listen to His voice?

Saul was rejected, not because he burned incense to glorify God's name, but because he was given a direct instruction, which he disobediently did not follow in the name of not trusting the outcome. Saul's disobedience can be traced to his desire to please man above God. It provides a powerful example of what the human desire for man's approval can lead to. (1 Samuel 15)

David had an adulterous relationship with Bathsheba which resulted in her becoming pregnant. He tried to cover it up by summoning her husband Uriah back home from the war and when he refused to leave the people of God, David had him killed. The child produced by that affair would later die.

Father, help us not to be so self-righteous that we disobey your direct instructions. We're trying to get revelation knowledge in Christ, because we want to fully know who He is to the capacity wherewith He is willing to reveal Himself.

Yet You've said to me, *"How can you know me if you don't study to show yourself approved? How can I reveal myself to you if you're not reading my word?"* (2 Timothy 2:15)

Even when we're displeased with the sequence of how events unfold in our lives, we need to still trust that You're working all things together for our good. We need to remember that we are married to you Lord. Nevertheless, there have been times when we've been unfaithful, and times we've played the harlot and fallen, but never from Your grace.

I've been an adulterous woman in my walk with God, I've slept with the enemy by entertaining him and allowing him to infiltrate my thoughts and my mind. On some occasions I've even allowed his voice to be greater than Your voice in that I acknowledge fear more than faith, failure more than victory, defeat more than deliverance, and focused more on the lesson than the love.

Perhaps this is why You say, *"Faithful are the wounds of a friend; but the kisses on an enemy are deceitful."* (Psalm 27:6)

I recognize if I'm not listening for Your voice, how can I ever hear it?

As Christians, sons and daughters of the most High God, we need to remember that although in the natural our vision may change, in the spiritual it always remains the same. God is not fickle, nor is He an *"Indian giver."* He never changes no matter how our circumstances may change.

And that alone should encourage you to close your eyes and see Him as He forever is.

When I first became a Christian, my whole ideology was shifted with the new understanding that there is a God who loves me beyond who I was or what I had done, and who was forever in my corner. It made me see life differently.

Life had new meaning and my outlook was favorable. I mean, "if God was for me, who could be against me," (Romans 8:31) is what took root in my heart. No opposition could prevail, nothing could steal my joy, no weapon formed against me could prosper ... right?

I need to know who You are so that I can know who I am. You have given me a name, You have set me apart. I am a princess, I am royalty, I am the daughter of the King.

Initially when trouble came, because it will come to us all, I bowed my knees and lifted my eyes, I sang victorious chants and jeered at the enemy who dared to come against God's elect ... and that sustained me, for a while...

Some contentions were stronger than others and some aversions lasted longer than others. And while some were futile and ineffective, others left scratches and gashes and scars. And over time, some scars were so deep they didn't have the ability to heal before the next affliction was inflicted, and as the days turned to weeks and the weeks to months and the months to years, without taking inventory, I became a shadow of my former self.

It appeared as though the well of my joy had run dry as I had been predestined to heartache and disappointments, false accusations and persecutions, chaotic dilemmas and ill treatment.

Salvation itself had seemingly lost its very power, and though I claimed to be "saved," I maintained very little attributes of that character – thus, I became a pessimist.

Truth is, I had always been one.

However, through the initial surrendering to God, I thought I had given it all up for hope. But subtly, without realizing it, I had taken back ownership of the very things I was once claiming victory over.

It became easier and easier not to pray, and if I sought God's direction, I never waited long enough to receive the instruction and in some ways was given over to a reprobate mind. Eventually I decided, all by myself, that God, in His infinite power and wisdom, had turned His back on me.

I rationalized that although I was one of His called, perhaps I was not amongst those that were chosen. I attempted several times to leave the church and God alone. Not to trouble or waste His time with my requests or desires, feelings He had decidedly taken the stance not to help me with or adhere to my pleas in lieu of all that I had suffered.

I reckoned it was better to leave His will, than to operate outside of it … but He would not suffer it to be so. Once you commit to God, He doesn't let go.

I fit nowhere!

I was no longer a part of the secular world's culture, but, in my eyes felt far from God's grace. So, I nestled into the humdrum routine of *"having a form of godliness but denying the power thereof."* (2 Timothy 3:5)

I had taken the stance not to cry anymore fruitless tears ... I asked not, I prayed not, I sought not, I expected not, I hoped not, I dared not, and I believed not ... therefore, I had not ... No expectations and no disappointments, and ultimately this course of thinking caused me to stop living, and merely exist. All too soon I began to practice religiosity and "Churchianity" rather than Christianity.

Now bear in mind as you read this that my focal point, which had started with Christ, culminated with "I."

There are two major errors I've come to discover that I made throughout this process.

The first being salvation wasn't about me. Every circumstance, pressure, test, and trial is not about you personally, but about God wholly.

All of my I statements demonstrated that I had made the process about me and not about Him.

"The name of the Lord is a strong tower, the righteous come in and they are safe." (Proverbs 18:10)

Acts 4:12 states, *"Salvation is found in no one else, for there is no other name under heaven given to mankind by which we must be saved."*

2 Timothy 1:9 says, *"He has saved us and called us to a holy life not because of anything we have done, but because of his own purpose and grace.* John 15:16 says, *"Ye have not chosen me, but I have chosen you ..."*

I forgot that *"to live is Christ and to die is gain."* (Philippians 1:21)

I forgot to *"count it all joy when you fall into various trials, knowing that the testing of my faith produces patience, and let patience have its perfect work, that I may be perfect and complete, lacking nothing."* (James 1:2-4)

I forgot to *"think it not strange concerning the fiery trials which come to try you, as though some strange thing had happened to me. But rejoice, in as much as we are partakers of Christ's sufferings, that when His glory is revealed, we may be glad with exceeding joy."* (1 Peter 4:12-13)

I forgot that *"if we suffer with Him, we shall also reign with Him."* (2 Timothy 2:12)

I forgot *"a servant is not above His Master and if they persecuted Him, they will persecute me also."* (John 15:20)

I forgot that *"greater is He that is in me, than he that is in the world."* (1 John 4:4)

I forgot that *"whatsoever is born of God overcomes the world; and THIS is the victory that overcomes the world, even our faith."* (1 John 5:4)

I forgot that I was *"crucified with Christ, nevertheless I live, yet not I but Christ that lives in me."* (Galatians 2:20)

I forgot to *"trust in the Lord with all my heart and lean not to my own understanding, but in all my ways acknowledge Him and He shall direct my path."* (Proverbs 3:5-6)

And most importantly …

I forgot that *"without faith it is impossible to please Him because he who comes to God must believe that He is, and that He is a rewarder to them that diligently seek Him."* (Hebrews 11:6)

You see, *"Faith is the substance of things hoped for and the evidence of things not seen."* (Hebrews 11:1)

"For if we have hope in this life only, we are of people most miserable." (1 Corinthians 15:19)

But I forgot my objective from the beginning, and I allowed the enemy (giving him no glory) to come against me with the very things that make me weak.

I strategized against myself and conceded to win by undoing the very foundation of my faith which was trusting in God. *"By which you are also saved ... unless you have believed in vain."* (I Corinthians 15:2)

So inadvertently I took my eyes off the solution and began to focus on my problems – and it became my very undoing. For while the trials were real, I lost focus of my redeemer who was well able to keep my foot from falling.

You see, whether the trials be of God for His edification or of the enemy geared for destruction, all roads lead back to God because He is seeking glory.

Yes, even what was designed for your evil is used by God to manifest who He is in you, not who you are in Him. The branches abide in the vine, and they only exist because of it.

The second mistake I made was to lack faith in God.

Did you know that the word "faith" is said to be mentioned well over three hundred times in various translations of the Bible?

As believers and Christians, we used the word to solidify our reliance and alliance to God based on what we know or understand about Him.

The bible states, *"faith is the substance (matured as fabric) of things hoped for, and the evidence of things not seen."* (Hebrew 11:1)

In other words, faith is the main ingredient in the recipe of salvation. *"He that cometh to God must believe that He is."* (Hebrews 1:6) (Acts 16:31)

"Believe on the Lord Jesus Christ, and ye shall be saved." Acts 16:31

Hebrews 11:6 also states that, *"without faith it is impossible to please Him."*

So, is God impossible to please without faith? Or are you?

How can you please someone you don't believe in?

Therefore, faith is imperative and necessary in order to move forward in God!

Help Me Remember

Father, I am the apple of Your eye.

The depth of Your love for us as Your children cannot be measured in height, depth, breadth, or width.

Before I was in my mother's womb, You foreknew me,

and called me to be a part of Your nation, work and family.

You know the plans that You have for me Father, to prosper me and give me a hope and a future.

Daddy, You care so much for me that even the very hairs on my head are numbered.

There is no limit to what You can and want to do in my life.

Help me to remember that if You are for me, who can be against me.

Help me to remember that You are my light and salvation, the strength of my life, of whom shall I be afraid.

Father, remind me that if You/God are for me, who can be against me.

Lord, help me to remember that You are slow to anger, that You prepare a table before me in the presence of my enemies and my cup runs over.

Father, I ask that You remind me that greater is Your spirit in me, than the part of me that's in the world, and that if You've begun a good work in me, You are able to perform it.

Daddy, remind me that I am the righteousness of God in Christ and that He sits as an intercessor and mediator on my behalf.

Father, help me to remember that I can honor You every day in everything that I do.

That I can be thankful for this life that You've given me that has hope and promise and unlimited potential to do great things when I submit myself to You freely.

All I have to do is remember who You are to me, and who I am to You, and surrender my will to Yours because there is no good thing that You will withhold from them that love You.

Father, remind me to honor You with my life, to worry about nothing, but with prayer and supplication, make my requests known unto You, for You know what I have need of, and You will supply them according to Your riches in glory, as long as they line up with Your good will and pleasure for my life.

You love me with an everlasting love, I am the workmanship of Your hands.

You breathed the breath of life into me and NO man can pluck me from Your hands.

I am Yours and You are mine.

I will remember to call on You because You will answer me, because You love me.

In Jesus' name I pray.

Amen.

Chapter 9: Knowing is Not Half the Battle, It IS the Battle

Often, as children of God, we speak with faith, professing His unlimited power and ability to do above and beyond what we can conceive in our hearts. (Ephesians 3:20)

Then, when we are confronted with seemingly "impossible" situations that we did not expect, could not predict or were not prepared for, we attempt to put our version of unconditional trust of God into action. However, if those expectations are not met with either quick results or the outcomes we were believing in, our facts become our truth and "The Truth" becomes unfathomable.

We transition from 'knowing' to 'believing,' and that belief can sometimes fail us.

Knowing who God IS, despite the circumstances, outcomes or "facts," can change your mind, life and perspective to such a degree that you are no longer motivated or weakened by what you see because what you know is greater than what you're currently experiencing.

And, *If All Things work together for our good* (Romans 8:28), and *the steps of a good man are ordered by the Lord* (Psalms 37:23) and *the plans He has for us are to prosper* (Jeremiah 29:11), and we KNOW this, why *faint in the time of adversity?* (Proverbs 24:10) Aren't we destined to *reap, if we faint not?* (Galatians 6:9)

Don't let what you think overshadow what you know!

Therefore, let us embark on a life changing journey as we propel our way, moment by moment, into our destiny; and it all begins with an initial first step. Make the decision to let today be that defining moment in your life.

Greater things ARE yet to come BUT ... it's time to be proactive in trusting and believing Our God IS who says HE IS!!

No more wavering, only steadfastness.

No more fear, only confidence.

No more defeat, only victory.

No more doubt, only faith.

No more indecisiveness, only assurance.

No more depression, only possession (of the things He has for us).

Lord, Help my unbelief!

Help me to know that everything meant for my demise will become my steppingstone and every tear I've shed will be replaced by unspeakable joy.

That each obstacle and disappointment of the past, present and future will become foundations of strength and platforms for someone else to stand on during difficult times.

May pain be turned to power and tests become testimonies.

We cannot be passive any longer, waiting for our circumstances to change; but rather we must take the bull by its horns and seize the day, relish each moment, and KNOW that if God is for us, who can be against us? (Romans 8:31)

Therefore, come to Christ with an open heart and bring as many empty sacks (spiritual) as your hands can possibly hold, because you're about to take back EVERYTHING the enemy stole from you (Isaiah 61:7, John 10:10, Joel 2:25) and receive new things that you never thought possible before this moment.

Are there people in your life who you know are true and dependable?

Are you one of those people? Now, can you imagine the hesitancy we feel towards one another because of the lack of relationship we've created with them?

In other words, because of the guilt and shame, WE purposely choose not to call on those we know are most reliable for fear of making them feel used or taken advantage of, so we choose not to call on those we know are most reliable.

Isn't that how we treat God as well?

We call each other brother and sister, yet we are easily offended, quick to cut one another off and sever ties, something we would NEVER do to our natural family members. So, let us remember to give each other room for "failure and growth," by showing love one towards another as this is the GREATEST commandment after loving Him.

"And by this they shall KNOW that ye are my disciples, if ye have LOVE one for another." (John 13:35)

Be dedicated to your relationships as He was dedicated to us and watch the beauty of Love (which can cover a multitude of sins) restore brokenness as it unfolds before you.

So let us gird our minds and cast down every imagination and every high thing which exalts itself against the knowledge of God and bring every thought into captivity of the obedience of Christ and learn to operate instead in love.

"WHAT DOES THAT MEAN?"

Don't let any thought that speaks against God's power, love, promise or capability fester in your mind or heart.

Try not to succumb to your emotions or feelings, depression, or defeat. Don't succumb to the desire to give up because things are difficult, challenging or appear to be out of control.

If God is not in **it**, don't entertain **it**, consider **it**, or give **it** credence.

Whose report will you believe?

We SHALL believe the report of The Lord!

And IF GOD be for us WHO can be against us?

Remember, God and you together are greater than a world of enemies that desire to knock you out and kick you when you're down; but the key is I/we must stand together with HIM. For greater is HE that is in ME than he that is in the world.

So, wash your face, comb your hair, and put your war clothes on! For the kingdom of God suffereth violence, and the violent take it by force!!! (Matthew 11:12)

Stand in the gap, keep praying, keep believing and surely God, in due season, will prevail in our situation.

The Bible says, *"But we are not of them who draw back unto perdition* (failure and punishment) (Hebrews 10:39); *but of them that believe to the saving of the soul"* (Romans 10:9), for we know who holds our tomorrow and we know who holds our hand. (Ecclesiastes 3:1-15)

God has promised us greater things and has given us a hope; let's not waste any more time in regret and doubt and fear because of things we "have known" to be the truth, but rather let us be hopeful and free from bondage as we move forward in the "absolute truth," that God loves us and He has a plan for our lives to give us a future and not harm us.

This is why it is so vital to understand that **knowing** God is able, is not the same as **believing** God is able.

I don't want to be controlled by yesterday and give any more power to those things that hurt me, that are gone and done with. I survived! I overcame it. I beat the odds. Despite the pain, I lived to see another day, another week, another month, another year, and more years ... so why would I give it the power to control or torment me.

Because I do not trust in God.

Oh, I believe in Him and understand that the world was formed by Him. And that all that exists, is by His hand. That He orchestrates Life and has me written in the palm of His hand. That He gives and takes away, allows people and things to come and go, all for our greater good.

His thoughts of me are to give me hope and a future, but I can't get past the journey that got me from there to here, or the failed dreams along the way.

How selfish and arrogant to judge the creator's choices because they didn't line up with my plans (as if I really had any).

And so instead I wallow, thinking about yesterday and never enjoying today, and forgetting that with tomorrow comes a better hope. Because He loves me, even if no one else does. And He's ever present, even when everyone else leaves ... but instead, I'm too consumed to notice.

Lord, Help my **belief**!

Help me to know that everything meant for my demise will become my steppingstone, and every tear I've shed will be replaced by unspeakable joy.

That each obstacle and disappointment of the past, present and future will become foundations of strength and platforms for someone else to stand on during difficult times. May pain be turned to power and testing become testimonies.

Hebrews 10:39 says. *"But we are not of them who draw back unto perdition; but of them that believe to the saving of the soul,"* for we know who holds our tomorrow and we know who holds our hand.

God has promised us greater things and has given us a hope, let's not waste any more time in regret and doubt and fear because of things we "have known" to be the truth, but rather let us be hopeful and free from bondage as we move forward in the "absolute truth" that God loves us and He has a plan for our lives to give us a future and not harm us.

Today is a new day and as we reflect on the inevitable changes that are ahead, we know that we are about to embark on a life changing journey. And yet, as we propel our way, moment by moment, into our destiny, we realize it all begins with today ... with an initial first step.

Greater things ARE yet to come BUT it's time to be proactive in trusting and believing Our God IS who says HE IS!!

No more wavering, only steadfastness. No more fear, only confidence. No more defeat, only victory. No more doubt, only faith. No more indecisiveness, only assurance. No more depression, only possession (of the things He has for us).

We can't be passive any longer in waiting for our circumstances to change. Now is the time to take the bull by its horns and seize the day, relish each moment and KNOW that if God is for us, who can be against us?

Your situation, my situation, our situations are nothing for God to handle. All He wants is our attention, loyalty, and faith.

He wants our dedication, our hearts, our trust, and He wants US to know NO-thing can pluck us out of His hands, for we are forever engraved in His palm! Come to Christ with an open heart and bring as many empty sacks (spiritual) as your hands can possibly hold, because you're about to take back EVERYTHING the enemy stole from you and receive NEW things that you never before thought possible. Don't give up on God, because He won't give up on you ... HE IS ABLE!

He Will Give Me a Song

Heavenly Father I want to thank you for the breath of life.

For being everything that I can ever think or imagine I need to be secure, happy, whole and complete.

You Abba are my strength!

In my weakness, You uphold me.

You carry me in Your arms, You cover me under Your wings, You nestle me to Your bosom.

You ensure that in times of weakness, Your strength is ever present to help lead and guide me.

Abba, You encourage me when I feel as though I can't move forward because of Your abounding love,

You guard my heart when I have carelessly left it exposed and vulnerable.

Your word says that You shield my heart.

When the elements of this life try to infiltrate it, then the cares of this life try to weigh it down, when I've trusted in man and they've failed me, when my hope waxes cold, when I fail to pray,

when I can't seem to find the strength to go forward.

You Abba are my shield.

You cover my heart with the pureness of Your love and sincerity of Your grace.

Lord, You give me a song in a strange and dry land.

You cause me to sing when my heart is heavy and has no melody.

You are the lifter of my head when my eyes hang low,

when tears well in my eyes, Father, Your whispers are the breath that dry them.

Lord, You gave me a song that the angels cannot sing, a song of redemption, a song of liberty and I will make a boastful noise, my heart shall hear thereof and be glad, because You will never leave me nor forsake me, You are with me always.

You guide my feet.

In Your infinite wisdom and grace You've held back nothing.

You gave of Yourself when there was nothing greater that You could give, Your son.

You are my rod and my shield, my protector, my hope.

Whether shall I turn to another?

No one loves me like You do.

No one.

What shall I say to these things?

If God be for me, who can be against me?

Therefore I sing because I'm happy, I sing because I'm free, His eye is on the sparrow and I know He watches me.

Thank you, Lord, for being all that I could ever think, need or imagine in Jesus' precious name, I pray.

Amen.

Chapter 10: It Doesn't Add Up

As children we were taught certain mathematical formulas that would be essential in figuring out the correct outcome/answer to certain equations. For instance, solving for the area of a triangle is obtained by multiplying the base by the height (A=bh).

However, to solve for the area of a circle, we would need to multiply pi (3.14) by the radius squared (A= I would say the latter equation is more complicated, especially depending upon the frequency by which you had to use it.

Now, if we were to delve into physics for a moment, equations can explain things such as mass (weight) being equal to density (thickness) multiplied by volume (how much), while also being equal to force divided by acceleration.

These "formulas" are essential to solving said equations adequately and as efficiently as possible and, through these and several other simplified consistent formulas like them, we are able to deduce one of two possible outcomes: identities and conditional identities.

An identity is true for all values of a variable, and a conditional identity is only true for specific values of the variable. And the equation is written as two expressions, connected by an equal sign.

Basically, a variable is an essential component to an equation that will eventually lead to its solving outcome. In the equation x=y, x and y are variables, and we understand that the values of those variables change according to our equation.

Thus, as students of the classroom, we were made to understand that all equations and problems have a rational, solvable end...

And therefore, as adults, we've applied such principles to our lives in order to deduce certain outcomes and control particular endings:

Two wrongs don't make a right;

Every action has an equal and opposite reaction; and

What goes around, comes around.

A set of equations with no conclusion is called inconsistent. Personally, I don't like math regardless of how essential it may be. Outside of knowing how to ensure I've received my correct change at the supermarket, or the correct discount at a 90% off Macy's sale, I'm fine.

Equations, for the most part, frustrate me, yet I use them all the time when dealing with God.

Let me demonstrate how I mistakenly used equations, which are inevitably a part of our lives, to SUM up God:

I mean, I could go on and on demonstrating ways that we've (or at least I've) interjected myself into God's equation to get a desired or expected outcome ... and failed.

Occasionally, there may be a fluke whereby happenstance we get the right answer, but the truth is we were never part of that equation in the first place.

Mathematical reasoning will tell us that an equation with no conclusion is inconsistent. That's what we, as humans, are unable to see – that all things are through the spirit, by the spirit, for the spirit, in the spirit. Therefore, save from prayer (in the spirit) we cannot come up with a consistent conclusion.

In considering these things, we must also factor in that God himself does not follow any particular formula to solve any equations pertaining to mankind. So, what does that mean or look like?

God solved Sally's problem like this (x) Sally's outcome was this (y). My problem is like Sally's, so: if I do this (x) it will come out like (y). If God does (x) like He did for Sally, it will result in (y) for me.

If God did (x) for me today and it resulted in (y) the answer, the next time I have that problem with God, I know that I can just apply the (x) method and we will come to the desired conclusion.

Know this, God rarely uses the same formula for the same person, much less for another person to get "the right answer," the same answer, or the same results.

The Bible says, *"Who can know the mind of God!?"*

In fact, the only equation I've ever seen God use consistently and universally was one that didn't make any sense at all:

It does not follow any rules, but it works every time, even when the variable is a flawed, inconsistent human being. And yet true repentance, void of change, cannot conclude the equation would read as such:

To make it untrue. These are two absolutes within the kingdom.

Joshua 23:10 states, "*One man of you puts to flight a thousand, since it is the Lord your God who fights for you, just as He promised you.*"

Deuteronomy 32:30 says, "*How should one chase a thousand, and two put ten thousand to flight, except their Rock has sold them, and the Lord had shut them up?*"

In Isaiah 30:17 it reads, "*A thousand shall flee at the threat of One.*"

In the Matthew 18:20 it says, *"For where two or three are gathered together in my name, there I am in the midst."*

These scriptures denote how the power of agreement and unity exponentially increases the odds in your favor when *two are walking together.* It also expresses God's promise to be in the midst of His people.

Thou Changest Not, but Your Method Does

Father, I thank You for being faithful and true.

I thank You for the holiness and truth that IS Your nature.

I thank You that You change not.

I thank you Father for watching over Your word to perform it.

You said it is because of Your mercies that we are not consumed.

Father, I know that You don't change.

You are the everlasting Father, the Prince of Peace, the Great I Am, the Lily in the valley, my Bright and morning Star.

When the enemy, even my foes come upon me to eat up my flesh, You cause them to stumble, when he comes in like a flood, You lift up a standard.

You watch over Your word to perform it.

You are mindful of me.

No weapon formed against me shall prosper.

I thank You Father because You don't change.

Even when You know that I fall short, even though You see that there is inconsistency in me, even when I think I know how You are going to respond and You don't You remain the same.

You lead me and guide me into All truth for Thy namesake.

It is because of Your mercy I am not consumed, great is Your love towards me.

Help me to trust that You will prepare a table before me in the presence of my enemies, help me to remember that You anoint my head with oil and my cup runs over.

You're watching over me and the word that You have spoken over my life so that everything that You have declared about me will come to pass.

In Jesus' name I pray.

Amen.

Chapter 11: New Wineskin: Change Your Garment

Joshua 9:12 says this, "Our bread was warm when we took it for our provisions out of our houses on the day that we left to come to you; but now behold, it is dry and has become crumbled. These wineskins which we filled were new, and behold, they are torn; and these our clothes and our sandals are worn out because of the very long journey." So the men of Israel took some of their provisions and did not ask for the counsel of the Lord."

Why didn't God allow the children of Israel to go into the promised land with the mindset they had?

"Why can't we have the old and the new?" Because new wine cannot be poured into old vessels, lest they burst! (Mark 22:2)

Each stage of our life in Christ is leading toward a transition and a steppingstone to the next level, and eventually all stairways lead to God. Sometimes roadblocks may be placed in our way to slow us down and deter us, while others are a flat out warning to keep away or go in a completely different direction, but we have to incline our ear (Isaiah 55:3) to know which way The Lord wants to lead us.

Not everything is the enemy or meant for evil, yet we're not totally in acceptance of God's plan for our lives, which makes the removal or cleanup process that much harder.

Remember when Jesus said, "He who loves his mother or father more than me is not worthy of me." (Matthew 10:37) In other words no circumstance, relationship or desire should supersede God's intended purpose and plan for our lives.

If you find yourself in a struggle or kicking against the pricks, compromising or doing things that don't edify the kingdom ... if you find yourself feeling lost or destitute or broken, chances are you're not yielding to God's perfect will for your life.

As I reflect over relationships and friendships forged, verified true, solidified faithful and suddenly lost, I realize unless God says it's forever, nothing really is.

You see, as children of the Most High we can get distracted in the beauty of friendship or the familiarity of a job or the comfort of consistency to the point where we're unwilling to let things go, see another way, or believe God for new things.

"Why can't we have the old and the new?"

Because, new wine cannot be poured into old vessels, lest they burst!

If you find yourself feeling lost or destitute or broken, chances are you're not yielding to God's perfect will for your life. Surely there are things in life we want or need, valuable relationships or treasures we hold dear...

Yet out there is a VAT of blessings, promises and new beginnings just waiting to be poured out, but ... we're too full ... of ourselves, of our past, of our wants, of our old ways, and there's no room for the new until we've been emptied out!

Let the Lord guide you in re-evaluating the inventory of your life.

Have you ever found yourself questioning God? Few, if any, can say no. And of those who take the stance: "God said it, I believe it and that settles it," I still believe there are times when they struggle with doubt or wonder what God is doing at a particular time in their lives when things just don't make sense.

Don't misunderstand me. It's a beautiful notion, to fully understand who the God of our salvation is and stand on His word, to know the vastness of His love and to grasp His intent for us in Him, but at times we get turned around.

The real truth is that whether we are seasoned Christians, new believers or just pondering His existence based on the things we have seen and experienced existentially, we have all found ourselves at one time or another in the position where we look at the world around us, and the things that are occurring in our lives, and wonder what God was doing.

In fact, if I were to be honest, since the time I decided to commit myself to the Lord, I've often found myself questioning why He chose me. I mean, if He's God and He knows all things, why would He bother with me?

I don't say this because I am some "terrible person" unworthy of God's love; and yet something deep within me feels so undeserving of His grace and confidence in me.

You see, in this new life in Christ, we've committed the worst atrocity to ourselves in that we've brought our old way of thinking and mingled it with the new, and neither one has a solid foundation.

Imagine for a moment that you're given a treasure map.

Most likely, it's a picture of a specific location, with a dotted pathway outlining a route that goes through plains and terrains, it crosses over territories and valleys riding a few rapids downstream, to finally reach the X marked out where the treasure lies beneath.

Many of us may look at that map and immediately think, "What's the quickest way, or shortcut, to get to that X?" or "How can I avoid all of this obvious unnecessary extra stuff and get right to where I need to go so that I can get the reward?"

Isn't that the way most of us think? We want to circumvent the process in order to get what we want. We want someone to make it easier for us, or we'll find a way to make it easier for ourselves. But it doesn't work that way.

The impeding problem that misdirects us from achieving this pathway to greatness, however, often lies within us, the recipient (as children).

We often respond to our natural parents in the same way that we approach God. We think to ourselves, "they don't understand," or "they're approaching things from their old way of thinking, but times have changed."

We don't realize that the map was created in such a way, that in order to make the next step forward, you need to have taken the last one behind. Any misstep in your approach can and often does send your navigation into reroute mode, trying to pinpoint your exact location, retrace your misstep, and take you back to the point of derailment so that you can continue your journey forward.

Know that *"The steps of a good man are ordered by the Lord: and he delighteth in his way."* (Psalms 37:23)

Outside of God's plan, there is no plan. Of course, we have free will to do as we please. However, if we desire to live for Christ the way He intended, we must be willing to listen, adhere to, and make adjustments based on His word and the directions He gives us through prayer, prophecy or that small still voice He whispers to us in the Spirit.

Empty Me Out

Father, I come before You in the precious name of Your son Jesus Christ.

I ask that you examine my heart and the thoughts that plague it.

Lord, remove everything that would hinder me from being completely dependent on You.

Lord, take away all doubts, insecurity, double mindedness, fear, envy and strife from within me. Father, You are my buckler, You are my truth, You are my protector, You are my keeper, You are my way maker, You are a promise keeper. Nothing is impossible for You!

Therefore, I ask that You empty me out.

Empty me from anything and everything that tries to usurp Your authority or cloud Your trust. Empty me from idols and priorities that I have made of man.

Empty me from the things that I have erected in my heart that nullify Your grace, word and truth.

Nothing is impossible for You Father.

All that I am or ever hope to be is found in You.

So I ask that You look at the things which I have valued above You and remove them from me, for I know that where my treasure is, my heart shall be also, and I desire to be with You.

Father, anything that hinders me or clouds me from seeing You, put it far from me so that I can build up treasures which the moths cannot corrupt, and the caterpillars cannot eat.

Lord, when I am empty, fill me up with You, for only You can supply all of my needs according to Your riches in glory.

Father, in the name of Jesus, I ask that you fill me to overflowing in the truth of Your word.

Help me to remember who You are so that I can know who I am.

Your buckler upholds the truth of who You are and the belt of truth that I need to walk in that truth.

Abba, I thank you for releasing every burden and the weight of sin which so easily besets me and for replacing it with the full freedom to serve You.

In Jesus name I pray.

Amen.

Chapter 12: Don't "Go!" Your First Love is Waiting on You

Isn't God amazing!

The fact that He foreknew us and predestined us from our mother's womb, all by itself, leaves me speechless and in awesome wonder of his goodness. We are *the workmanship* of His hands, chosen for His purpose, separated for His glory.

He told Jeremiah, *"Before I formed you in the womb, I knew you; before you were born, I sanctified you..."* (Jeremiah 1:5)

David said, *"You created my innermost parts. You knit me in my mother's womb."* (Psalms 139:13)

Paul stated it this way, *"But God, being rich in mercy, because of His great love with which He loved us, even when we were dead in our transgressions, made us altogether alive in Christ."* (Ephesians 2:4-5)

Every so often we need to remind ourselves that *we did not choose God, but rather He chose us.* (John 15:16) It's necessary that we understand this, otherwise we feel that we have some sense of entitlement as if God owes us something, or that He needs us to accomplish His will. He DOESN'T!

He is God all by Himself!

"His grace is sufficient for me," and without Him my fate will be failure if I don't fulfill His purpose.

The Father does not need me, I need Him, but yet He wants me and loves me. I am the apple of His eye. Another concept that floods my soul with overwhelming warmth, and more often confusion, is that He wants me!

In Jeremiah 31:3 he says, *"I have loved you with an everlasting love; I have drawn you with unfailing kindness."*

He said to Isaiah, *"Behold, I have engraved you on the palms of my hands." (49:16 ESV)*

"...Even the very hairs of your head are all numbered. Fear not therefore: ye are of more value than many sparrows." (Luke 12:7)

So, the question remains: if we were predestined, fore chosen of God, called by name, and separated by the Father to be His own, who is it that He *DOESN'T* know?

Is there anyone He CAN'T know?

As the omniscient (all knowing) God, is it possible for Him NOT to know someone?

Most of us would say No!

However, in Matthew 7:23, Jesus states on judgment day that the Father will say *"I declare to them, I never knew you; depart from me, you workers of lawlessness."*

How is this possible?

How can He tell us that He knew us before we were formed in the womb and later say I never knew you?

Is God forgetful?

Did He lie?

His word cannot return unto him void; therefore, how can the creator of humanity not know His creation?

The Bible says our first responsibility is to love the Lord: ... *"You shall love the Lord your God with all your heart, and with all your soul, and with all your mind, and with all your strength."* The second is this, *"You shall love your neighbor as yourself. There is no other commandment greater than these."* (Mark 12:30-31)

Therefore, the question remains, what does it mean to love God with all your heart, soul, mind, and strength?

It means to trust in Him explicitly. To give him everything. To seek Him always.

Some of us trust in horses and some in chariots; some trust in jobs and paychecks; some trust in stoplights and highway lines; some trust in the governmental systems and politicians; some trust in social security and medicare; some trust in the economy and it's welfare system; some trust in house locks and security gates; and some trust in husbands and wives and children, while others trust in the world system, but Joshua said, *"As for me and my house, we shall trust in the Lord."* (Joshua 24:15)

I believe that to lose sight of our first love, is to forget that, in *"Him we move and breathe and have our being,"* (Acts 17:28) for *"apart from Him we can do nothing."* (John 15:5)

Again, we see in yet another scripture where the bridegroom rejects the five foolish virgins stating He did not know them.

"While the bridegroom tarried, they all slumbered and slept. And at midnight there was a cry made, Behold, the bridegroom cometh; go ye out to meet him. Then all those virgins arose and trimmed their lamps. And the foolish said unto the wise, Give us of your oil; for our lamps are gone out. But the wise answered, saying, Not so; lest there be not enough for us and you: but go ye rather to them that sell, and buy for yourselves. And while they went to buy, the bridegroom came; and they that were ready went in with him to the marriage: and the door was shut. Afterward came also the other virgins, saying, Lord, Lord, open to us. But he answered and said, "Verily I say unto you, I know you not. Then shall the kingdom of heaven be likened unto ten virgins, which took their lamps, and went forth to meet the bridegroom. And five of them were wise, and five were foolish. They that were foolish took their lamps and took no oil with them: but the wise took oil in their vessels with their lamps." (Matthew 1-25)

This phenomenon always befuddles me. How could He not KNOW them?

What exactly made these virgins foolish? Were the ten not all "saved," were they not all chaste, were they not all set apart for the bridegroom, did they not all fall asleep?

Many preachers and teachers of the gospel have suggested that the rejection of the bridesmaids in Matthew's parable is due to their lack of preparedness for the bridegroom's arrival. The symbolism expressed by their lamps running out of oil can plausibly serve as an adequate interpretation that they were spiritually depleted or otherwise unprepared to receive their groom. This may also further imply that they had lost the presence of the Holy Spirit altogether, explaining why they weren't ready at the time of His arrival.

This interpretation offers an almost plausible explanation for why they were left behind. However, that the bridegroom would declare, "Depart from Me, I do not know you," seems like a harsh response to that negligence.

What exactly is the Lord saying to us when using this parable as an example, if all scripture is profitable for reproof, correction and training?

Is He imploring us to be watchful? To be found waiting? To always be prepared and in expectation for His arrival? Did He require "full lamps" as a prerequisite to come into His presence? Why didn't the five foolish virgins think instead to just follow behind those who had light? Couldn't they all have made it to the bride chamber walking closely together? And being that they had all fallen asleep, why weren't the wise virgins rejected as well?

To leave these questions unresolved contradicts the very concept of a merciful and long-suffering God and may raise deeper questions about the nature of grace and under what circumstances it is extended.

What we do know is that despite their shortcomings, these foolish virgins would come into recognition, albeit late, that they needed more oil in order not to miss His arrival.

The suggestion to "go to those who sell" was at that of the wise virgins, who beckoned them to get more of their own oil, as they would not share what they had, fearing what they had would not be enough to carry them through. This event is what actually caused them to miss His ultimate arrival.

Nevertheless God assures us that we are inscribed on the palms of His hands (Isaiah 49:15–16) and that He would never forsake us, so how do they then become forgotten and unknown by Him?

I want to propose two speculations: The first is that because He is Alpha and Omega, the Beginning and the Ending, the First and the last, that He knows us, truly knows us. He's always KNOWN us. In other words, because He is all knowing and all seeing, and considering that we are spiritual beings having a human experience, I believe that God also knows our expected end and what is required to fulfill our purpose in Him.

In other words, the only way He cannot know us, is when we don't fulfill our purpose therefore we become foreigners to God.

Which brings me to my second conjecture. It was common in Jewish tradition for the oil lamps to be held by spinsters who stood behind the bridegroom to ward off evil spirits, and therefore oil lamps weren't necessarily a requirement for marriage.

So my second speculation is this: Is it possible that perhaps the real problem wasn't that they didn't have extra oil or even a little oil at all, but instead the fact that they chose to heed to another voice that wasn't the Lord's?

Yes, we have to be very careful to ensure that we are not prepared to receive the bridegroom when He comes, but we also have to understand that we need to recognize His voice when He calls.

We have to take heed where we stand, less we fall, but we also have to be cognizant that even if we have flaws, we can bring them to the throne of grace for only He can redeem us from the enemy and ourselves.

John 10:27-28 says, "*My sheep hear my voice, and I know them, and they follow me: And I give unto them eternal life; and they shall never perish, neither shall any man pluck them out of my hand.*"

In Matthew 25 it says, "*at midnight there was a cry made, Behold, the bridegroom cometh; go ye out to meet him.*" The voice directed them to **Go meet Him**, but instead they heeded the voice of the virgins who told them **to go and buy**, and so they disregarded the directive of the Lord and went to replenish what was lost.

There are so many Christians that walk in fear of falling more than they are aware of the path that they are on therefore it deters them from ever really getting closer to the Lord.

There are so many Christians that are following churches, preachers, teachers and heeding to other voices more than they are willing to follow the one and true living God because they're more concerned with what people think, than God.

Our love for God must supersede anything we may desire to do or seek. We have to be willing to walk in darkness until He lights our way.

Do you believe that Jesus is God? Do you believe that He is just a part of God's word or all of God's word? Because you question the things He says to do, you inevitably question the God whom you say you serve. When your mind yields to the flesh, it takes someone who is completely pure to save you from the flesh.

How then can you know Him?

How then can He claim to know you?

Jesus said, "*Whoever will confess Me before men, him will I confess also before My Father who is in heaven.*" Matthew 10:32

I believe the ultimate answer lies in Revelations 2:2-5, "*I know your works, your toil and your patient endurance, and how you cannot bear with those who are evil, but have tested those who call themselves apostles and are not, and found them to be false. ³ I know you are enduring patiently and bearing up for my name's sake, and you have not grown weary. ⁴ <u>But I have this against you, that you have abandoned the love you had at first.</u> ⁵ Remember therefore from where you have fallen; repent, and do the works you did at first. If not, I will come to you and remove your lampstand from its place, unless you repent.*

Do you recall when you first received Christ into your heart and got saved? Do you remember how it felt – as though you were breathing for the first time and your love for Him was so overwhelming you were willing to follow Him through the rough terrain of the mountain top and the steep slopes of the valleys?

Let us evaluate our true first love.

Are you currently in a relationship or were you ever in a relationship before? Can you recall the feelings you had when you thought about that person?

When you're committed to someone, they're usually all you can think about first thing in the morning, last thing at night, and every waking moment in between.

You spend quality time together and speak frequently on the phone or in person, always seeking a way to be with the object of your affection. But over time, we tend to take these relationships for granted as we familiarize ourselves with the person, we become complacent!

Dates and phone calls become less frequent, and that happy giddy feeling goes away all too soon. Life settles into a routine and the spark seems to fizzle over time until the thrill and excitement of that love seems to die.

My brethren, this is how we treat God.

Initially, when we first came to Christ, we were zealous, hopeful, and dedicated. I used to wonder how I ever breathed without Him, walked without Him, lived life without Him.

But all too soon everything we do concerning God becomes monotonous and habitual, just like our feelings for people dies down, and eventually because *of life,* we become less dedicated, motivated, and less interested in pleasing Him.

Our expectations begin to flounder because of past experiences, failures, and defeat, and ultimately doubt and uncertainty begin to take residency in a once hopeful heart.

But we need to render our minds towards greater things, greater dedication to prayer, God's word, discipleship, and Ministry.

And let's not forget to add enhancing, not deflating, our relationship to that list. Let us be more committed to God and the things of God. Let us rekindle our first love ... first towards Him and then others.

Are there people in your life who you know to be true and dependable?

Are you one of those people?

No one can imagine the hesitancy we sometimes feel towards one another for fear of rejection or the lack of relationship we've created with them because of lack of trust.

In other words, because of our guilt, shame, or previous disappointment, we impose restrictions on ourselves. We call ourselves concerned about making someone feel used because we only call on them when we're in trouble, subsequently choosing not to call on those we know are most reliable.

This is how we begin to treat our Heavenly Father.

Where is the love in that?

Where is that faith in Him that He alone is the God of our salvation?

Let us remember that we need to give other's room for failure and growth by showing and giving unconditional love towards one another as this is the greatest commandment after loving Him.

"You shall love the Lord your God with all your heart, and with all your soul, and with all your mind, and with all your strength. The second is this, You shall love your neighbor as yourself. There is no other commandment greater than these." (Mark 12:30-31)

Remember therefore the seasons in your life where you went *back for more oil* yourself, as you squandered through the darkness. Repent, ask for forgiveness and rekindle the fire in your heart for Him. Therefore, *"Rend your heart and not your garments."* (Joel 2:13)

He's waiting on you.

Hope in God

Oh my soul why art thou disquieted within me, hope thou in God?

Lord, I trust in You.

Even when I face circumstances that I don't understand because I know that You want the best for me.

You said that Your plans are to give me a hope and a future.

Father, sometimes the way seems dark.

Sometimes it appears as though there is no positive way out of certain situations

… and yet, it can't be true because Your word says that You would keep me in all of my ways

You said that You want to give me the desires of my heart.

You said NOTHING shall be impossible to them that believe.

You said that You would never leave me or forsake me.

You said that You love me more than I could ever think or imagine.

So when I am faced with difficult times and I feel as though I'm helpless and hopeless, help me to remember that You are a VERY PRESENT help in the time of trouble.

Help me to keep my eyes fixed on You and to seek You first and all other things shall be added to me.

Help me to remember that You are not a man that you should lie and if You said something, You will bring it to pass.

You said that You complete the work that You've started.

Oh my soul, why art thou disquieted within me, hope thou in God.

Father, I know that You are able to supply ALL of my needs according to Your riches in glory.

And that Your strength is made perfect in my weakness.

Show Yourself mighty and strong in every circumstance and situation I face, both great and small.

What shall I render unto You Lord for all Your benefits towards me?

Father, I beseech You on behalf of Your mercy and grace and unfailing love.

I ask that You step into each and every circumstance that I face, whether good or bad.

Teach me to try the spirit and know that it is You.

I thank You for my family and those people in my life to help guide me towards my destiny and strengthen me in You, but I Pray that their voice never supersedes Yours.

I even thank You for those who would try to derail me because it is an opportunity to prove Yourself faithful and true.

Father, I thank you Lord for meeting and supplying each and every one of my needs according to Your riches in glory.

Watch over my children Father, keep my marriage strong on Your foundation, save my loved ones, heal those that are sick or suffering from sickness whether physical, mental or emotional.

Father watch over these leaders of this world and nation.

Give them a heart that reflects Your heart Gives us, as a people, ears to hear what You say and eyes to see Your desire and design for us.

Father, help us not to follow a stranger.

Father, lead us and guide us into all truth for thy namesake.

I believe Lord, help thou my unbelief.

In Jesus' name I pray.

Amen.

Chapter 13: Be Like Thomas, but Don't Let Them Change Your Name

Through the simple deception of focusing on one's self-perception rather than God, the enemy has caused the people of God to suffer from an identity crisis. Whether we think too highly of ourselves or less than we ought to think. By infiltrating our thoughts and sowing seeds of self-righteousness he has defrauded the children of God into believing who they are in Christ is determined by what they do, rather than understanding that He has established who we are because of who He is and not because of what we do.

In fact, from the very beginning of creation the enemy has deceived man and led him astray by pointing out his flaws and shaming his nakedness, causing man to fear and hide from God. Despite creating man in His image, breathing life from his own breath into him, giving him access to and placing him in charge of all that he had created, and talking and walking with him daily, man has chosen to disregard all that God has established with him, to listen to the voice of the enemy, and God, recognizing that man's reply was far from what he had founded in him, asked the question: *"Who told you that you were naked?"*

So many times, we listen to voices other than the Lord's, and He simply wants to know who told us what we are currently believing?

Psalms 11:3 asks a pertinent question: *"If the foundations be destroyed what shall the righteous do?"* That foundation has been the principal establishment of God's word and promise which stands sure.

Galatians 2:16 reads, *"Knowing that man is not justified by the Works of the law, but by faith in Jesus Christ, I do not set aside the grace of God, for if righteousness comes through the law, then Christ died in vain."*

Without the spirit of God, it is easy to be misled by the enemy. All of life's experiences will teach us that in the natural world, this is how they respond to failure and shortcomings.

This is why Paul implored that, *"Christ may dwell in our hearts by faith, that being rooted and grounded in love we may be able to comprehend with all the saints what is the breath (width), and depth (deepness), and height (measurement from the base to the top), and know the love of Christ, which passes knowledge that you might be filled with all the fullness of God."* (Ephesians 3:17-19)

It is a simple deception of self-perception the enemy seeks.

In other words, God's love for us has no measurement, no container, no limit, and no natural understanding. Even if you could imagine or fathom the expanse of God's vast love for us, we would fall short to genuinely comprehend the Infinity of its reach. This kind of understanding can only come through faith.

Now the Bible states that God has dealt to every man a Measure of Faith and like that parable of the talents, we are required to increase that Faith by learning to trust and see God's hand through the life experiences we encounter. Remember, "*Faith is the substance* (heart) *of things hoped for* (expected), *the evidence* (proof) *of things not seen* (unknown, unsure)." Hebrews 11:1

Therefore, he (you) who comes to God must believe that He is God-able, capable, willing, loving, forgiving, and that He is a rewarder, promise keeper at, and giver of them, you that diligently, purposely, actively, vigorously, and eagerly seek him, otherwise it is impossible to please him.

The easiest translation of "please" in this scripture would be to make happy.

If you had a relationship with someone, and you never trusted them to be honest, faithful, caring, giving, or loving, what kind of relationship would you have?

Could you please that person?

Would that person please you?

Of course not, because the opposite of faith is distrust, the opposite of belief is disbelief, the opposite of security is doubt, acceptance is rejection, optimism is skepticism, clarity is confusion, certainty is uncertainty, initiation is hesitation, and blind faith is questionability.

Needless to say, if we functioned in our natural relationships and experiences the same way we functioned with God, we would have no relationship at all because the tendency would be to push away, not to draw closer.

When I originally understood this scripture, I automatically thought, "it's impossible for me to please Him, so why bother," being that I was operating in doubt at the time. I erroneously took that impossibility as God turning his back on me, rather than having a broken heart for my rejection of Him. Herein lies the heart of self-centeredness. When we look at the problem through our eyes rather than the eyes of God, it is the simple deception of self-perception.

But what happens when it's not you who is speaking negatively?

How do we counteract the names, curses and titles given to us by others which don't align with God's word?

And this brings me to Thomas, whose name was Didymos, both which mean twin. Though it is not mentioned that he had a twin, it is speculated that he may have mirrored Christ in his purpose for ministry. The Bible also doesn't mention what his profession was (however, it is believed he was a carpenter just like Jesus). Nonetheless, we know that he was a Greek man, chosen by Jesus as a disciple to follow Christ from the very beginning, and what may not be known is that he remained faithful to his calling even after the end.

So why is it that this man of God received the label (nickname) *Doubting Thomas,* that many call him to this day? Thomas, sadly has received a bad rap, portrayed as though he was one who was not as dedicated to Jesus as perhaps the other disciples were thought to be. He has become the representation of faithlessness or doubt, which is far from who he truly was.

Thomas was so dedicated to Jesus that when the other disciples warned Him not to return to Judea because the Jews had conspired to stone Him to death, knowing that there was a threat against Jesus' life, Thomas alone says, *"Let us also go that we may die with Him."* John 11:16

Thomas is also the disciple who inquired during the Last Supper, *"Lord we do not know where You are going. How can we know the way?"* John 14:5 This prompted Jesus' explanation that is believed of us all today, that salvation comes through God alone.

So how did Thomas get the name he is known as today, *Doubting Thomas*?

After the resurrection of Christ, He appeared to a group of disciples, but Thomas was not among them (John 20:19-24) and later when it was told to him, he responded by saying *"Unless I shall see in His hands the print of the nails, and put my finger into the print of the nails, and thrust my hand into His side, I will not believe."* John 20:25

That proclamation would forever be the defining moment in Thomas' life for many who read this passage.

But isn't that just like the devil? To label us according to where we fall short instead of acknowledging where God is taking us? Isn't it he who is constantly reminding us of our past and present mistakes as a way of keeping us distant from God?

Doesn't the Bible implore us in Matthew 7:1-3 to *"Judge not, lest ye be judged. For with the same judgment ye judge and with the same measure we measure, it shall be measured against you."*

Would you like to be remembered or known as Lying Sally or Unfaithful Frank, especially after you've surrendered your life to Christ?

Are we not human, trapped in this sinful flesh? Prone by nature to go against God ... *"But God, who is rich in mercy, out of the great love with which He loved us, even when we were dead through our trespasses and sin, has made us alive together with Christ; for by grace are we saved."*

Sometimes we're quick to identify a person's shortcomings rather than identify their needs. Sometimes we lack sensitivity. We need to be available to help someone else's needs besides our own so that God can use us.

And when Thomas did see Jesus, he alone acknowledged His deity by stating, *"My Lord and My God,"* because he recognized that they were one in the same. *"Flesh and blood hath not revealed it unto thee, but my Father which is in heaven."* Matthew 16:17-19

Peradventure, the Father allowed the prompting of this question for those of us who might later question the validity of Christ's resurrection, or commit the error of offense, yet need mercy.

What if Thomas asked the question because he too wanted another experience with the Lord, knowing that He is no respecter of persons, and had appeared unto the others?

Thomas was a faithful servant, and although the Bible does not mention his whereabouts after the day of Pentecost, in the latter part of his life he would be the only disciple to go on to minister in India and later China, bringing the gospel to many, which now have the foundation of Christ through his life's teaching and sharing the gospel.

If this is true, this would mean that his influence has impacted more people than any of his fellow disciples, yet he is not remembered for this. Instead, he is known as *Doubting Thomas*, a name that doesn't suit him, an unfair representation of his true calling and fulfillment of purpose.

No one ever really discusses the fact that when Mary said she had seen Jesus at the gravesite where the stone was rolled away, the disciples thought it to be untrue. Nor do they mention that Jesus appeared to the other disciples, which is why they believed and could attest to the fact that Christ was risen. For true faith is *"The evidence of things not seen."*

When Jesus said to Thomas, "Blessed are they that have not seen and yet have believed," He was referring to us, not Him, but the statement couldn't have been made if He had responded any other way.

Imagine for a moment what could have happened if Thomas was deeply offended and wounded by that label given to him?

Imagine what would have happened to Thomas if he chose to internalize that title and said to himself, "there's no point in continuing because look at what the people think of me?" Think about the legacy and the ministry he would have left behind because of what people may have thought about him.

Now imagine for a moment that YOU were defined by your greatest mistake. Think how you would feel and operate in God knowing you were constantly being referred to as a thief, or a liar, or a fornicator, or an adulterer, or a blasphemer?

Would You be able to continue ministry without offense, knowing that you were being addressed by something you did, rather than who you are or were meant to be?

Change your name, and don't respond to someone naming you something you are not or that God didn't call you.

Don't allow the world to name you when God already named you. When your image lines up with God's word, nothing will be restrained.

We are already victorious. Our assignment is on earth, but our citizenship is in heaven.

I am becoming more and more aware that I am not responsible for the personal development of any Christian I know or have a relationship with. My dedication is to God. To share His word. To be Christ's hands, feet, and mouthpiece.

I have a personal opinion on things I see or have experienced, especially those that are offensive to me, but while those experiences may be real, my opinion is invalid. No matter how offended I am by words, deeds or wrongdoings perpetrated against me, my position to judge or hold malice is unjustifiable.

Romans 14:4 states, *"Who art thou that judgest another man's servant? To his own master he standeth or falleth. Yeah he shall be holden up: for God is able to make him stand."*

God will not be mocked, He will repay ... so why would I choose to hold bitterness or unearth my peace in defense of the Gospel?

It is Christ that died.

God doesn't need a lawyer, He needs representatives who will stand in the gap, love as He loves and hope as He hopes.

We are called to maintain our position, uphold the name of Christ through godliness and pray for those who "despitefully use me and say all manner of evil against me."

I know many of us have experienced such judgment, whether fairly or unfairly, nonetheless God is the only true Judge! You are more than the sum of your choices, greater than the weight of your failure, higher than the position you stand right now and more powerful than the weakness you possess.

Remember, it is better to fulfill your calling in the face of laughing people, than to miss your destiny to those who don't care about the course your purpose must follow.

I Have Overcome the World

Father,

You are my strength and my refuge, My fortress, my God in whom I trust.

Father, as I think about the trials and circumstances that come to press me in this life

I realize that everything that happens is a part of Your purpose and Your plan.

Jesus said, "fear not for I have overcome the world."

In other words, tough times are a part of the process, but they all lead to a greater good.

I am victorious, circumstance does not dictate my position in heaven nor who You called me to be on earth.

I am more than a conqueror.

That's who I am, no matter how much I seem to fail, no matter how far I think I've fallen from grace, no matter how insignificant I feel.

I am more than a conqueror.

My responsibility is to believe it, embrace it, and live in the fact that I am who You say I am and not what I think or others say I am.

God is a deliverer and He will deliver me from anything and everything that tries to destroy me if I trust in Him.

Afflictions are not for my destruction, they are for God's edification and glorification.

He is using my pain to build His reputation as a deliverer, comforter, healer, reviver, restorer, redeemer.

He is a VERY PRESENT help in the time of trouble so I can rest assured knowing that when I am facing tribulations and tough times that He is closer to me than I could ever imagine, delivering me from evil for unto Him is the kingdom and the power and the glory forever.

God is a deliverer!

I thank you for all that you've brought me through, and all that you've helped me to overcome.

Father, You also gave me my name, I am beautiful in Your sight I will not let anyone take that from me or even when I fall I am still the righteousness in Christ You know my name. and yet You love me just the same.

When I fall from grace, It is You alone that picks me up.

You restore my soul when my well is empty.

I thank you for Amazing Grace.

In Jesus' Name I pray.

Amen.

Chapter 14: Guard Your Heart!

I have learned, and whatsoever State I am, therewith to be content. I know both how to be abased and how to abound everywhere, and in all things I instructed both to be full and to be hungry, both to abound and to suffer need. I can do all things through Christ to strengthen me.
Philippians 4:11-13

I have discovered that as Christians we are undone through our carnality. The pursuit of our personal desires requires us to think a certain way which allows the enemy to find a foothold in our life.

Paul stated, *"For me to live as Christ and to die is gain."* Philippians 1:21

In other words, this life that I live, I live unto the glory of Christ, but should I die, I win because I will be with the Lord in glory.

Well, favor, blessings, and gifts are from the Father. We lose sight that He is not obligated to fulfill our every desire or what we consider need. All that He does for us He does out of love as long as it aligns with His will, plan and design for our lives. He will not do anything outside of His timing or purpose.

Have you ever found yourself in a position where it seems as though God has forsaken you?

A place where you cry out to Him, and He appears to be far from your voice?

We have labeled those experiences as a dry place or the Wilderness, but what exactly is a wilderness experience?

If we recall the story in Exodus, the children of Israel entered into the Wilderness after crossing the Red Sea. The parting of the Red Sea represents Grace and Power in its most perfected form, demonstrating the capability of our God.

However once in the wilderness, the Israelites began to murmur and complain, desiring natural expectations such as water and bread, and while God willingly obliged their desire, they were perpetually unsatisfied, seeking more provision with disregard to what God had already supplied and provided for them thus far.

The wilderness, in essence, represents that place where our personal desire tries to impose an obligation on God to fulfill our wants, whether they be in or out of His will, yet not considering either.

Why is it that we try, whether consciously or unconsciously, to force God's hand to give us what we want?

The answer is simple. Carnality!

We live in the flesh, and we seek all the natural comforts that would satisfy its yearning, whether that be food or clothing, shelter or passions, power or wealth, recognition or appreciation, health and wholeness and the list goes on and on.

Essentially, we are never appeased because once we have what we've asked for, we move on to the next request.

Now, I'm not saying that it's not God's objective to see us whole or complete, and having every essential need. However, He stated that He wishes above all things, that we should prosper and be in health, even as our soul prospers. 3 John 1:2

But how exactly does our soul prosper, seeing that personal Prosperity must be intertwined with spiritual gain.

Adam and Eve had dominion over all the Earth. Everything made by the hand of God was available to them, at any time, except for the fruit from the Tree of Knowledge, which happened to be the catalyst the enemy used to gain a foothold in their life.

Why?

Because he cajoled them into thinking about the one thing God refrained from them rather than appreciating all that He had given them.

Isn't that just like the enemy – to point out the things we lack, disregarding the reasons why we don't have them and making us focus on the why or the how to acquire that thing or those things, rather than recognizing that if God wanted us to have it, we would.

Didn't he say in Romans 8:32, *"He who did not spare His own Son, but gave Him up for us all, how will He not also, along with Him, graciously give us all things?"*

But Paul, in Philippians 4:11-13, sought to teach us a great lesson. He stated, *"Whatsoever state I find myself in...,"* in other words, rich or poor, hungry or full, healthy or sick, wanting or satisfied, married or single, I learned to be content.

Notice, he said learned, not simply "I am," as if to imply some unnatural phenomenon, something that he was born with or adapted to as a conclusion. Learning comes from experience, and experience teaches.

Assuredly, at the beginning of his journey as a new convert fully committed to Christ, he may have had some expectations to be received with open arms. After all, he was a changed man filled with all scholarly knowledge of God, understanding circumcision and the laws of God, yet converted from a persecutor to join the cause for Christ.

However, that was not the case at all. Instead, he was in prison and beaten several times, shipwrecked, in danger for his life, he suffered sleepless nights, hunger and thirst, and experienced cold and nakedness. He was rejected and persecuted by both Jews and gentiles. He endured feelings of worry, anxiety, weakness, and daily pressures. 2 Corinthians 11:23-29

But through it all, he learned to trust in God and depend upon his word, through selflessness and wanton abandonment for his own desires, wants and needs.

You see, the secret to Our Success is simple. It requires us to believe in God for everything while simultaneously accepting, not for conformity but for endurance, whatsoever circumstance we find ourselves in, knowing that in due season, or when the time is right, we shall reap if we faint not. Galatians 6:9

How can the devil unearth you if you are not moved by anything he does because you trust, that despite your present situation, God is working out your life behind the scenes, especially if we understand that all things work together for good to them that love God, to them who are called according to his purpose? Romans 8:28

Now that's a secret with sharing!

Be anxious for nothing, wells, power, recognition, love, understanding, acceptance, success, health, materialistic gain, forgiveness, justification, acknowledgment, gratification, help, clarity, freedom, favor, blessings, or anything that would require us to seek the acceptance of man and the validation of the flesh.

But in everything, all things, all situations, all circumstances, by prayer and supplication, seeking God's will, with thanksgiving, knowing that God is able, let your requests, desires, appeal, proposal, suggestions, proposition, be made known to God and the peace of God which surpasses all understanding, will guard your heart and minds. Philippians 4:6-11

Guard your heart and mind?

Against what?

Against thoughts and persuasions of the tempter that will tell you that you have to have it; need it now; why isn't God doing it for you; He doesn't love you; He doesn't care what you're going through; He's forgotten about you; He isn't real; He's rejected you; you sin too much; you've gone too far; you're not good enough; you're not pretty enough; you don't deserve it, and other such foolish and distorted thoughts that come flooding into our minds to make us doubt or give up.

For once these things get into our hearts, they are very difficult to combat.

Proverbs 4:23 tells us to, "G*uard our heart with all diligence for out of it flows the issue of life*." Our heart is the essence of who we are and the motivator of the things we do. Therefore, if we are not careful, through our own desires and conceits we can be led astray, deceived, and even destroyed.

What's In My Heart

Father, I love You.

I thank and praise You for considering me.

Before I was formed in my mother's womb You knew me and yet You still called me Your own.

Father, I am beseeching You on behalf of my heart, for out of it flows the issues of life.

My heart is heavy Lord.

It is filled with words I cannot utter.

You said that You know my thoughts afar off.

You said You heal the broken hearted.

You said that it's the things that come out of a man that defile him for evil thoughts, murders, adulteries, fornication, thefts, false witness, blasphemies … come out of man but those things are conceived in the heart.

This is why You've asked me to guard my heart, so that I might not sin against thee.

In John 14:1, *You said let not your heart be troubled.*

The psalmist David said, *"Create in me a clean heart and renew a right spirit within me."*

Today I am asking that You reveal the deep things concerning my heart.

Heal me from hurts of the past, experiences that tried to break me, thoughts that seek to overtake me and make me feel worthless.

Remind me that I Am Your child.

Your thoughts of me are good.

You want to give me a hope and a future.

You want me to succeed.

Ephesians 3:17 says, *"That Christ may dwell in your hearts through faith, that being rooted and grounded in love, I may be able to comprehend what is the width and length and depth and height of Your love towards me which passes all knowledge that I may be filled with all the fullness of God."*

Lord, I'm asking that You search out the things and thoughts that trouble me and excavate them out from the root of my heart so that I can be made whole.

Forgive me for all doubt, unbelief and double mindedness.

From everything that I allow myself to separate myself from Your mercy and grace.

Uphold me with the right hand of Your righteousness and lead me into Your peace and truth so that whatever is in my heart reflects Your word and love towards me.

In Jesus' name I pray.

Amen.

Chapter 15: Change Your Mindset

"Be not conformed to this world, but be transformed by the renewal of your mind, that by testing you may discern what is the will of God, what is good and acceptable and perfect". (Romans 12:2)

Have you ever watched a television program or documentary on any eating disorder?

Diseases like anorexia and bulimia nervosa both have similar traits wherein one's perception is thwarted.

In both illnesses, the affected person believes themselves to be heavy when they're actually not, which in turn causes them to starve themselves or binge eat and purge the food through drastic measures. In most cases young girls and women see a contorted view or image of themselves in the reflection of the mirror and in response to this try, by any means necessary, to lose weight.

That perception of themselves is so powerful it has the ability to make a skinny person, that may even be down to just skin and bones, see themselves as fat and overweight. However, it's not so much what they see when they look at themselves, but how they react to what they see that affects them. For in response to the reflection, drastic measures are taken as a means to remedy the problem, which can result in anything from starvation to extreme sickness and even lead to even death.

Unfortunately, there is no easy solution to remedy the illness because the solution is strictly dependent on how the person perceives themselves. The issue becomes exasperated when no measure of dieting can ever help that person feel secure enough to feel as though they've achieved their ultimate weight loss goal. In order to achieve the perfect image, or accept that sometimes not so perfect image, they must first change their mindset and how they perceive themselves.

Using a different example, we know that a baby grows in its mother's womb, for the gestational period of nine full months before being ready to enter the world. Initially, the child has plenty of room to grow, stretch, and develop, but over time as the infant matures and grows to full term, the allotted space becomes more and more confined. Eventually, the baby will conform to the restricted space, and uncomfortably make adjustments within that area by balling up into what is known as the "fetal position," by positioning his knees in close proximity to his face.

However, in due season, the womb, which cannot withstand the continued inward development of the infant's weight or size, begins to contract, literally forcing the baby out into the world. It has to do this because the baby is not trying to leave, despite his limited motility.

Once in the world however, despite that limitation of space has been removed. Nonetheless, the child, remaining unaware of his new surroundings and spatial availability, continues to abide balled up tightly and constricted as though he is still in the womb. He must reform his way of thinking, so to speak, in order to understand he is no longer restricted and confined to that small space.

As Christians, we too must continually grow and renew our mindset in order to adapt and change our way of thinking to adjust and expand, as God enlightens us and downloads new knowledge and seeks to clear away old concepts.

Oftentimes as children of God we are faced and challenged with times of adversity, denial, rejection and/or limitations within our human means. Our reaction, most times, is to rescind and retreat, metaphorically balling up into a fetal position, which tends to bring us the most comfort in our painful situation. We use it as a way to shut the world out around us.

If we are not retreating, we can also often find ourselves questioning our stance in God, God's love for us and all the why's and what's in between. These mostly skewed perceptions (like the eating disorder) can cause us to restrict our diet in Christ where we find ourselves reading the word less and praying less frequently as well.

This, most often, is how we deal with or react to problems and situations we cannot control, and while, for the most part, it's okay to initially respond this way, if after careful evaluation, pondering and seeking the Lord's direction we choose to continue on the current trajectory, the problem exacerbates itself when we try to remain this way as a means of self-preservation, locking ourselves off from meaningful human interaction and Godly connection.

And we know that living constricted and confined, alienated from life, love, and friendships does not mimic the freedom and peace that Christ came to give those who were captive in their minds and wounded in their hearts. In the Bible it says, *"He was wounded for **our***

***transgressions**, He was bruised for our iniquities: the chastisement of our peace was upon Him; and with His stripes we are healed."* Isaiah 53:5

In other words, the punishment, beating and mental anguish that Christ endured was so we could have peace in any, and all seasons of our life – even hardship. This is the beauty of the bloody cross … He came to free us from the bondages of sin.

God wants us to know Him as much as it is possible, through the spirit, for He is our Father, and we are His children. He is an ever-revealing God. Sovereign and wise in all his ways, mindful of us.

Each trial, situation, and circumstance we face is specifically geared and designed to shape us and mold us into the person we are designed to become. And while all circumstances are not created by God, for many, situations can be traced back to a poor decision we ourselves have made.

The all-knowing, ever-loving God we serve is able to use each and every circumstance to bring His name glory, and ultimately elevate us to the next level in trusting in who He is.

Have you ever heard of the expression take the limit off God?

That simply means stop confining God to the image you can conceive of Him in your small finite mind. God's ability goes far beyond what you can imagine or think or read or hear. It has no height, depth, or width wherewith one can humanistically measure, conceive, perceive or understand. And yet, many of our experiences, which are meant to draw us nigh unto God, usually requires us to separate from ourselves and from our own way of thinking in order to do so successfully.

Now, where this might seem like a simple solution, one might be amazed at the difficulty of this undertaking. If you've ever placed a spoonful of food, that was slightly hotter than you expected, into an infant's mouth, it's almost impossible to convince that child to take the next spoonful, even if it has been properly cooled. And why is that?

Because the condition of the mind of trust has been broken, and once this occurs you might have to almost let the food get iced over, in order to regain the child's trust again.

The same can also be true of a bad eating experience. One bad experience at a food establishment can forever taint your impression of that establishment to the point where even the thought of eating there turns you off.

So, like children and patrons are we. Once scorned, burned, misled, hurt, taken advantage of, and broken, our level of trust is diminished, if not all but depleted, and the idea or notion of revisiting such a traumatic event, seems overwhelming.

And yet the God, who is not at the source of the problem, but still held us throughout the problem, is now being blamed for the length of time it took to resolve the problem or the fact that we even had a problem in the first place.

So many misconceptions fortify the untruth of God's lack of care for us, and in turn, we rescind into a ball and withdraw from God and the world and hurt, to protect our fragile psyche from being further damaged or taken advantage of.

But who really was to blame?

The Bible specifically tells us to be transformed by *renewing our minds*, and that how one perceives, so is he. And what that simply means is everyday must be faced as a new day with endless possibilities and opportunities in Christ, or if not be subjugated to the false ideologies of the enemy. (Romans 12:2; Proverbs 23:7)

The way to renew our mind is by reading God's word in order to reiterate God's promises, so that we can see ourselves the way God sees us and not how we see ourselves. To understand that in this life we WILL have difficulties, nevertheless we will overcome even as Christ overcame. John 16:33

Too often we allow the changes around us to change what God has placed in us!

We must remind ourselves that just because we can't feel God, it doesn't mean He's any further away from us than when we did feel Him.

The same holds true that knowing God is able, is not the same as believing God is able.

Many times, as children of God we speak with faith, professing His unlimited power and ability to do above and beyond what we can conceive in our hearts. Then, when we are confronted with seemingly "impossible" situations that we did not expect, could not predict, or were not prepared for, we attempt to put our trust in God into action, and usually fail.

Nonetheless, if our expectations are not met with either quick results or the outcome we were believing God for, our facts in circumstances that do occur, become our truth and *"**The Truth**"* of who God is, becomes unfathomable because we rationalize our truth and experience against who God states that He IS.

We go from knowing ... to believing, and that belief can sometimes fail us.

But Knowing who God is, despite the circumstances, outcomes or "facts," can change your mind, life and perspective to such a degree that you are not motivated or weakened by what you see, because what you know is greater than what you're currently experiencing.

If All things work together for our good, and the steps of a good man are ordered by the Lord, and the plans He has for us are to prosper ... and we KNOW this, why faint in the time of adversity?

Aren't we destined to reap if we faint not?

Don't let what you think overshadow what you know!

Therefore, as we reflect on the inevitable changes that we know lie ahead, for we know that we are about to embark on life changing events, let us remain focused on the God of our salvation. As we propel our way, moment by moment, into our destiny, we realize all the more, it all begins with today ... with an initial first step.

Greater things ARE yet to come, BUT ... it's time to be proactive in trusting and believing Our God IS who says HE IS!!

No more wavering, only steadfastness.

No more fear, only confidence.

No more defeat, only victory.

No more doubt, only faith.

No more indecisiveness, only assurance.

No more depression, only possession (of the things He has for us).

We can't be passive any longer in waiting for our circumstances to change, but rather we must take the bull by its horns and seize the day, relish each moment, and KNOW that if God be for us, who can be against us?

Your situation, my situation, our situations are nothing for God to handle but He wants our attention, He wants our loyalty, He wants our faith, He wants our dedication, He wants our hearts, He wants our trust, and He wants US to know NO-thing can pluck us out of His hands, for we are forever engraved in His palm!

Come to Christ with an open heart and bring as many empty sacks (spiritual) as your hands can possibly hold, because you're about to take back EVERYTHING the enemy stole from you and receive New things that you never before thought possible.

Don't give up on God, cause He won't give up on you ... He is ABLE!

We must keep in mind that transformation is not instantaneous, and although God can change our minds in an instant, we are usually required to go through a process of re-conforming our minds.

This process requires us to be diligent in His word and constantly thinking about what we are thinking about, and filtering those thoughts through the word of God to see if they align with His word.

We want to be careful not to give up too easily or be too harsh on ourselves while going through the process, for setbacks will come. But instead, we must be patient and long-suffering as it took some time to develop such a mindset. It will take some time to transform it.

Remember that God is for us throughout this transition, and it is His prompting that gently nudges us to evaluate where we are so that we can progressively move forward to the next level in Him.

Be encouraged, be blessed, and change your mindset.

Direction from God

My help comes from the Lord, the creator of heaven and earth.

My Father knows what's best for me and can lead and guide my footsteps, save my loved ones, heal the sick, encourage the downtrodden and supply all of my needs according to His riches in glory.

I can do all things through Christ who strengthens me and upholds me.

Father, be my help at this moment and every moment of my life.

Strengthen my heart to know that You care for me and desire to give me the best.

Help me to seek You always for all things.

Daddy, I need you to be with your children right now, speak to your sons. Enlighten their minds.

Send them a Divine visitation where they can sense Your presence and direction.

Lord, do what You have to do to get their attention and redirect their path.

Lord speak to your daughters.

Pull down the strongholds of the enemy that try to bewitch their minds.

Let us know whose we are.

Father, cover each and every one of your children. Keep us in Your care.

Cover us by Your grace.

Lead us in the plain paths for righteousness sake.

Perfect the work that You have begun in us.

Lord, continue to bless and keep the work of Your hands.

Use us for Your glory and honor. Put a hedge of protection around us to keep us from all hurt, harm and danger.

Father whatsoever the enemy meant for evil, turn it around for Your good.

Let the words of my mouth and the meditation of my heart be acceptable in thy sight.

In Jesus' name. Amen.

Chapter 16: Sometimes You Just Have to Wipe and Flush

"Even today my complaint is bitter; His hand is heavy in spite of my groaning. If only I knew where to find him; if only I could go to his dwelling! I would state my case before Him and fill my mouth with arguments. I would find out what He would answer me, and consider what He would say to me." (Job 23:2-5)

Some things in life you can't control the outcome of no matter how hard you try. Despite our best efforts to procure a specific end-result, especially in certain situations, sometimes things just don't play out as planned, no matter what one strategically does or doesn't do.

Oftentimes, we can find ourselves revisiting the drawing board in our effort to salvage a dream, by meshing it with a new one, while valiantly avoiding the decision to give it up altogether. It is a noble gesture of faith unrealized, fueled by our relentless desire to achieve the goal we are striving for.

But what happens when the efforts of trying to achieve those dreams come with a hefty price?

What happens when the thing that we are striving for, and simultaneously failing at, causes more heartache than seems bearable to endure?

A failed marriage that you put your heart and soul in to save, a lost relationship after years of dedication and trust, an unachieved goal in which you sacrificed time or money, a job in which you gave the very best of yourself, or a sickness that has wracked your body in spite of prayers, that caused you to shed blood like tears only to not attain your expectations despite your pleas?

Anyone who has ever been through anything that is painfully heart wrenching and emotionally exhausting knows it's not just a matter of picking up where you failed and starting again. It takes courage, it takes determination, and it takes patience, all with an unspoken willingness to pick up where you left off and try again. And though it takes much bravery, no one speaks about the fear.

Fear is a powerful mind gripping emotion that can maneuver itself through the smallest sliver of doubt, and if you're not careful, fear can overtake your desire and stifle it until it becomes unviable. The Bible says, "*Fear has torment*," and truth be told, it is the opposite of faith.

Now, I asked this question once before, but what do you do when faith dies? How can you proceed forward in boundless trust when it is mixed with uncertainty and doubt?

Nonetheless this is how God wants us to trust Him. He wants us to live each moment believing that He is always able and willing, above all else, to do anything and everything, despite anything we may have experienced prior to a failure or success – and do it fearlessly. This is the best manifestation of faith over fear.

But again, it may sound easier than it seems ... or maybe not. Because of our human nature, our propensity to fall prey to fear is easier than our willingness to believe, and that is most often how the enemy strikes. In Job 3:25, he states, *"For the thing which I greatly feared is come upon me, and that which I was afraid of is come unto me."*

Our fears have the ability to take on a nature of their own and spiral into something more than we could have ever imagined possible, making it harder to recover what was lost or left behind. In fact, fear left unchecked will become dangerous to overcome, causing us to doubt God's goodness and abort His plans. Fear, left to its own devices, will manifest in sickness and mental distress.

So, what do you do when you're facing fear? You face it with God! You tell Him how you feel and expose where your unbelief is. Ask Him to help you. Tell Him how much you want to trust Him but need His help. Fear that is felt in secret is a breeding ground for the enemy to produce guilt; and guilt produces shame, and shame pulls us away from God and His promises.

A few years ago, my husband and I were trying to have a baby. Although we already had a daughter together, I knew my husband wanted a son. Since my previous pregnancy was so difficult, he resigned himself to be content with the one child that we did have together (plus those I already had), but I believe he did that in an effort to avoid disappointment.

Nonetheless, as many may be astutely aware, most women won't settle for simply resigning Not being able to do something, and being who I was, I had already decided we would have a son.

Being that I was determined to get pregnant on my own, I wanted the doctor to clarify with 100% certainty that it would be completely impossible for us to get pregnant if we continued to try on our own in order to determine our odds of our being successful, and he concluded that we only had a 1% chance to produce a viable pregnancy without intervention. He also interjected that if by chance we did conceive, we had a 50% chance of miscarrying or producing a child with some kind of genetic complication.

So here were my odds: 25% chance to get pregnant via medical intervention or 1% chance of conception on our own with a 50% chance of either losing that pregnancy to miscarriage or a 50% producing a genetically disabled child.

To his conclusion I instinctively responded, "What you're saying is, other than a miracle, there is no way for me to get pregnant on my own?" And his response to me was, "Not a miracle, a 1% chance", to which I replied, "That sounds like a miracle to me!"

It was devastating news, nonetheless I knew that with the God that we served, nothing was impossible! It was at this point I asked the doctor if he had ever been wrong in his conclusions and his response was that he had been doing this for twenty-five years and he knew his craft; however, there had been a small few, who, despite his expectation, did conceive. And it was at this juncture I told him to prepare a space on his wall for me, because I was going to be the next one to prove him wrong.

Within the first three months we got pregnant for the first time, however 9 weeks later I began bleeding and ultimately miscarried. Six months later we would conceive again and this time I would carry the pregnancy to 11 weeks only to be told at a prenatal visit that they could no longer detect a heartbeat. In lieu of this my doctor wanted me to have a D & C to remove "the fetus", but I was still hopeful that he was wrong so I refused to have the procedure done believing that by some miracle, they would find a heartbeat when they checked me again. I would be wrong.

When I went to the doctor for a follow-up visit a week later he would haphazardly state he was relieved that my body had gotten rid of it on its own and that I was no longer pregnant. It was heart wrenching to hear and painful to accept. Both my husband and myself were devastated. But in the middle of our disappointment I turned to my husband and said that perhaps God allowed me to get pregnant to prove to us that he was able to overcome the 1% odds against us, but what we desired had to be within His timing.

Little did we realize that four years would pass without another pregnancy and then in March of 2016, after I had all but resigned that I would never have another child, I found out I was pregnant for the third time.

Ironically, I had always stated that I would not be willing to have another child past the age of 45, but please know that our Father has a wonderful sense of humor and will sometimes challenge us by our words. I was actually three months into my forty-fourth birthday when I found myself pregnant again.

However, at this juncture I was terrified. In fact, I wish I had never discovered I was pregnant again because I didn't want to experience another disappointment that came with losing another child.

Secretly I was anticipating another miscarriage, simply because it had happened twice before, therefore every time I went to use the bathroom I would look into the toilet expecting to see blood as I had in the previous two pregnancies before.

This hadn't been something I'd ever had to deal with before trying to get pregnant on purpose, but nevertheless because of my experience and the doctor's declaration it became something that I had grown accustomed to expecting.

Then one day I heard God ask me a question, "Will you trust Me?"

I wanted to, but fear had taken its claws and dug them deep into me, nevertheless I knew that I needed to trust Him implicitly, I just didn't know how to trust Him with this situation anymore. In my heart I said, "How can I do that and not be afraid?" And He simply told me I just needed to believe!

The bible says in James 2:14 *"What good is it, my brothers and sisters, if someone claims to have faith but has no deeds? Can such faith save them?"* It further goes on to state in James 2:17, *"Even so faith, if it hath not works, is dead."*

So from that moment on I took the stance that despite what I had been through, despite my experience, despite my age, despite what I had been told, despite what I expected I needed to trust God and from that day forward, every time I went to use the bathroom, I decided I would just wipe and flush.

As crazy as it sounds, looking into the toilet represented doubt, looking into the toilet represented fear, looking into the toilet represented that my faith was relying on what I could see therefore I decided I had to have blind faith and trust that no matter what happened from this point forward I was going to trust God! The results were nothing less than miraculous. Not only did I conceive four years after I had already been told that my eggs were too old, I would also carry this pregnancy to full term, and would give birth to a healthy baby boy two months shy of my forty-fifth birthday.

God took that 1% probability and used it to demonstrate that with Him, nothing is impossible to those that believe.

Is there something that you are believing God for or have been hoping for that has not yet come to fruition?

Is there something that you believed God for and despite waiting and hoping, the outcome was not as you expected?

Have you been devastated by a dream that almost manifested but the end result didn't fulfill what you desired? I am here to tell you that you are not alone, many have been in your position before you, but I am also here to let you know that God is the only one that has the final say.

In fact, as I wrote this testimony a dear friend of mine's mother was extremely ill and everyday her prognosis was getting worse. Then the doctor gave the family that dreadful report no one wants to hear, that she only had months to live. As a family they were believing in God, yet from the daily deterioration of what my friend saw, hope appeared to be blocked from fully manifesting itself.

Fear and a bad report was trying to take hold of her and although I tried to encourage her, fear secretly kept saying that the worst was inevitable. Then one day God reminded me of my journey through faith and nudged me to share it. No, our situations were not the same, but we served the same God, the God of the impossible!

Determined to help strengthen her faith I told her my story. I made her understand that we cannot go by what we see, despite how real and overwhelming it may seem. Trusting God for a miracle means we have to use our eyes of faith. I encouraged her to keep trusting God and if she had to go into that hospital room and cover her eyes in order to hold onto faith, to do so. This was her wipe and flush!

The end of her story hasn't been written yet, but we know that no matter what, God has the final say, not man. But remember, He's looking for unadulterated faith. That is what moves mountains, that is what changes circumstances, that is what produces miracles!

So, does that mean if you can't believe implicitly that God won't do it for you?

The answer is: not necessarily. Remember, our lives are living epistles being read by all those who surround us daily and see and experience our walk with Him. God knows the ending from the beginning, and He is seeking to get the glory from our lives any way He can. He knows that people are living vicariously through us, seeing how we, the children of God, respond under pressure and amidst devastation and disappointment. We are to be beacons and our light is to shine before all men that God our Father may be glorified.

Yes, it's easy to doubt when the odds are stacked against you and your back is against the wall. Yes, it hurts to believe for something, especially when the conclusion is not what you are expecting. Yes, it's hard to keep the faith when history has already written a story of failure. But remember God is not a conformer. What happened yesterday does not determine what God can and is doing today. The results that others may have experienced in the same situation does not necessarily tell us what our outcome will be, only God can determine that.

But oh, the satisfaction to take God at His word and see Him fulfill His promise! Oh, the glory that God receives if He decides to lean in your favor and show you off before all the world to see. Oh, the honor that can only be felt by a heart that held on to see the end results, in spite of the odds.

My dear sister, my dear brother, I am imploring you to trust God, perhaps in a way that you never have before. He wants to do it for you, and He wants to get the glory. I am imploring you today, no matter what the situation, no matter what you are believing God for, to wipe and flush and keep it moving, trust Him blindly, trust Him fearlessly, trust Him hope-fully, trust Him until He says No, and believe that He will come through for you, because that is the kind of God that we serve and there is no better way. For we know that if He CAN'T do it, it CAN'T be done! And there's NOTHING He CAN'T do!

Rest in You

Abba,

Father and creator of all things, I look to You for strength and peace and rest.

You alone are my comforter.

You alone are my refuge, I desire You to clear my heart and mind from anything and everything that tries to cloud, distort or impede my view from seeing You in absolute and complete control over my life.

Nothing will happen by accident.

Every circumstance and situation is strategic and purposeful to making me into who You're calling me to be.

I trust the process because You are the processor.

All things are working together for my good and today I embrace what You are doing to secure that my steps are in line with Your will for my life.

The heavens declare Your glory, the earth is Your footstool and I am the workmanship of Your hands.

I praise the God of my creation, I praise my Father who gives hope.

I love you Father, because You first loved me and my desire is to rest in You because in Your arms there is no lack.

I thank you because You see me and know me and still You call me your own.

What more security can I need?

Lord it seems so mystifying and alluring to think of you as this ominous untouchable being who is so perfect and pure, yet just outside the grasps of humanity's reach.

Father you are omniscient, omnipotent, omnipresent and yet a man who can be touched by the feelings of our infirmities.

The creator of the universe, serving the universe, that was created by Him and all for the sake of love and redemption, who could phantom such a perfect plan of redemption.

To be the healer and the cure both for the sake of elevation, justification and glorification.

Everything we need all balled into one for the saving of our soul and the healing of the nation.

Too complex to be understood too simple to be believed.

How great is our God!

You, Father, are the Godhead bodily and peace for in You dwells all.

You are good and Your mercy endures forever.

Father, I come to You today asking that You continue to direct my path, order my steps and give me the strategy and the strength to do what is necessary for me to walk in victory.

I thank You because You have equipped me with everything I need to be an effective parent, spouse and witness to Your name.

You know the struggles and trials I face on a daily basis.

I pray that You continue to help me navigate every circumstance so that You get the glory.

I pray for wisdom that gives me insight and the will to do what is needed.

My desire is to trust in You and believe that NO-thing will be impossible to him that believes.

I thank you for the strength and faith to believe You when the odds seem against me, because You are the God that will never fail, and you have the final say on all things.

Therefore I rest in You, knowing that you are mindful of me.

In Jesus name I pray.

Amen

Chapter 17: The Other Side, A Journey Through Faith

"How long will you waver between two opinions? If the LORD is God, follow him; but if Baal is God, follow him."
(1st Kings 18:21)

Isn't it amazing how as believers, one minute we can be found in the midst of miracles, seeing the power of God move and know without a shadow of a doubt that He is real and can do all things but fail, yet as we continue living life, removed from those miracles we begin to question His ability to save and deliver.

At some juncture in our lives we are inevitably confronted with problems, situations, circumstances, illnesses, tragedies, or frustrations that challenge and put to the test the faith that lies within us. The very faith we once had because of the miracles we saw walking with God, and sadly many times our meter comes up short.

It happens to the weakest of us, it happens to the strongest of us. It happens to both seasoned and unseasoned Christians. Those who have called down the power of God and those whose hands have received miracles, to those who have seen the fig tree (something that God removed from our lives that was not productive) dry up at God's word.

Life can find a way to inundate us with difficulties that seem to have no quick, easy or obvious solution and we are only left with the resolve to trust God.

There are countless stories within the Bible that tell us accounts of righteous, God-fearing believers and prophets that felt they were too insufficient and insignificant to carry out God's will:

Abraham lied about Sarah being his wife.

Moses struggled with a speech impediment.

The spies of Israel gave a report of impending defeat.

David wanted acceptance.

Job cursed the day he was born.

Gideon believed he was too weak.

Elijah wanted to die.

Isaiah said he was undone.

…and the list goes on and on.

None of these men of God had encountered or walked with the latter promised Messiah, nor experienced His miracles firsthand, like the disciples had. Simon Peter, was amongst the first to be called.

In Matthew 16:18 it reads, "And I say also unto thee, that thou art Peter, and upon this rock I will build My church; and the gates of hell shall not prevail against it." When Jesus called Simon He immediately changed his name to Peter because although we may not be able to see anything significant within us God knows who we are and who He created us to be.

He is able to see our ending from the very beginning. This is how and why he chooses what may appear to be foolish or nonsensical to others and calls them to a position that places them a powerhouse in the Kingdom of Heaven on earth.

In Luke 4:38, we find Jesus in Simon's house, where He not only healed his mother-in-law from a fever, but in Luke 4:40-41, it states that all they that were sick and with diseases came unto Him, and He healed them and devils came out crying.

Later In Luke Chapter 5:1-3 we find Jesus standing by Lake Genneserat where there were two ships but no fisherman to be found. In fact, they were washing their nets after fishing all night and catching nothing and Simon Peter was one of those men. If this is true this would mean that Simon Peter wasn't home to witness the miracles that had taken place at his house.

As the verse continues the story tells us that Jesus enters Simon's boat and asks him to thrust out onto the waters where He sat and taught the people on the shore. After His sermon, in Luke 5:4, Jesus asks Simon to *"Launch out into the deep and let down his net."*

And in Luke 5:5 Simon responds, *"We have toiled all night and caught nothing, nevertheless at thy word I will let down the net."* This would mean that Simon Peter wasn't home to witness the miracles that had taken place at his house.

I'm sure at this point they were tired, I'm sure they were disappointed. Could Jesus offer insight to something they were well acquainted to and accustomed to that would prove different from what they had already experienced?

One might presume that Simon and his shipmates, as fishermen, were well seasoned and knew what they were doing; after all, this was their profession and livelihood. evertheless, they took heed to His words and decided to try again.

Perhaps they sought to test His words and see what He would do or perhaps they complied only to illustrate their own point. Whatever the motivation, Peter chose to obey Jesus even though there was no rationale or other directives behind His words.

This result is not typical of many of us? We rarely consult with God when we think it's concerning what we already know or are familiar with.

In Luke 5:6-8 we see that a great multitude of fish were caught, and that the catch was so great that they had to beckon to the other ship on the shore to come and assist them and both ships were filled to the point of sinking.

It is therefore incumbent upon us to recognize that although God can provide the clarity needed for us to take action, He often leaves us without enough detail to feel completely comfortable, as we tend to desire too much information in order to move at His word. Instead Peter chose not to question the reasoning behind jesus' request, even if he secretly believed he knew the likely outcome, after all they HAD toiled all night without success.Isn't this true of many of us?

We rarely consult with God when we think it's concerning what we already know or are familiar with.

In Luke 5:6-8 we see that a great multitude of fish were caught, and that the catch was so great that they had to beckon to the other ship on the shore to come and assist them, and both ships were filled to the point of sinking.

Isn't it amazing how God uses this opportunity to affect all four of the fishermen with one miracle? And ironically Jesus sent them back to the same side they had exhausted themselves on all night. Isn't this just like God to take a situation that looks hopeless and perform a miracle!

In reality the principle that Jesus was demonstrating is that it doesn't matter what you think you know or who goes with you, if God is not ordering your steps or leading the way, we're on our own.

In that pivotal moment, Simon realizes his own inadequacy in the face of Christ and exclaims, "Depart from me, for I am a sinful man."

In truth, Jesus proved that it doesn't matter who goes with you, because if God doesn't, we're on our own. And it is here, in this very moment, Simon recognizes that he is insufficient among the Christ and says, *"Depart from me for I am a sinful man."*

To understand the majesty and sovereignty of God is to recognize that, in His presence, we are undone as sinners and insufficient before Him. It is only He that qualifies, cleanses, and justifies.

In Luke 5:10 Jesus tells those very same men that from henceforth they shall be *"fishers of men"* and they need no more convincing, leaving all to follow after Him because they want to see what else He is capable of.

And from Luke 5:12 through Luke 7:21 we read of multitudes that were healed and delivered. A leperous man, the man with palsy, He ate with publicans, healed a withered hand, healed diseases and those vexed with unclean spirits, the Centurion's servant, the widow woman's only son was raised from the dead, He cured infirmities and plagues, cast out evil spirits and gave the blind sight. And during all of these wondrous acts the disciples were there to serve as witnesses of the miracles that Jesus performed.

In Luke 8:22 it reads, *"Now it came to pass on a certain day, that he went into a ship with his disciples: and he said unto them, Let us go over unto the other side of the lake. And they launched forth."*

Matthew's account would be similar and also document in chapter 8:24 that a tempest arose while they were on the boat and Jesus was in the gally asleep. And the disciples being frightened, awakened Him and asked the question: *"Carest thou NOT that we perish?"* and immediately He would speak to the winds and waves and cause them to cease.

So where is Jesus when He's silent in the storm? The answer is He's still in your boat and He's resting assured because He's still in control.

Pay attention to His words, *"Let us go to the other side."*

God can't lie and God can't fail, yet they went to Him Last instead of first.

Jesus, Don't you care about what's happening in my life? Don't you see the storm I'm facing right now? I believe that this is a question many of us have asked at some point during our walk with Christ and He is still speaking into our situations and causing the winds and rain to cease. He wants us to rest assured in Him, which is why I believe He was fast asleep.

Jesus used this situation to demonstrate not only His connection to the Father and His deity, but also His abounding love for us and the knowledge that no matter what is going on around us, He's always with us.

If this weren't enough in Matthew 14:29, Jesus walks on water towards the boat and Peter, afraid, asks, *"Lord if it is You, bid me to come."* Isn't it interesting that Peter calls out Lord? This indicates that he knew it was Him, but just wanted reassurance, and yet when He responded all He said was *"Come."*

God doesn't have to give much instruction: *"come, go, peace be still"*… we only need to trust Him and the process will play itself out. Notice how Peter only begins to sink after taking his eyes off Christ and placing on the turmoil around him? <u>Remember</u> Peter was a fisherman by trade, he had faced many storms <u>before this one</u>. In fact in Matthew 14:24 it states, "But the ship was now in the midst of the sea, tossed with waves:for the wind was contrary."

The sea was already in turmoil when Peter stepped out of the boat, so why did he become afraid when the winds became boisterous? Because he was focused on the wrong thing.

<u>The same Peter</u>, in Matthew 18:21, it is Peter who asks the question, *"How often are we to forgive our brother?"*

I believe that the answer to that question was not only for us to recognize the need to forgive others, but for Peter's sake, so that he could also extend mercy to himself. Although he didn't know it yet, he would later deny Christ and be devastated with guilt, but God foreknowing, chose to communicate His grace and mercy towards the man upon whom he would build His church by intriguing him to ask this question that would later be pertinent to himself.

In Mark 16:7, Jesus, Moses and Elijah appeared before Peter, James and John in the mountain of transfiguration allowing them to experience Christ's divinity and dominion so that there was no mistaking His deity and who God had called Him to be.

In John 6:68, Peter says to Jesus, *"Where else shall we go seeing You have the words of eternal life."* Here Peter acknowledges that Christ's teachings and preachings were life transforming.

Don't you find it interesting that one moment Peter is saying, "Lord I am ready to go with You, both into prison and death" and not shortly thereafter find him denying Him? That scripture is followed up by stating but Jesus, knowing all that was in his heart stated, *"Peter...the cock shall not crow this day before thou shalt deny me three times."* (8:22, 8:34)

I have always wondered why Peter was able to deny Christ three times, and I came to realize that each denial represented something that each of us struggle with today: doubt, fear, and self-identity.

In the midst of miracles and wondrous things taking place, there was still doubt among them. There was doubt after everything they had experienced. There was doubt in spite of being with Jesus. As Christians and believers, we've walked with Christ, prayed in His name, seen the manifestation of Him making ways out of no way and still, when the next difficult thing presents itself, we

w.o.n.d.e.r., ... we have questions, we feel anxiety, ... we have doubts.

He witnessed his teachings and miracles firsthand and yet, in the face of adversity, he withdrew, fearful of the repercussions of being associated with Christ. When he was approached several times by various people who knew that he had been with Jesus, he was alone, sitting amongst the crowd wanting to be with Christ, close to Him, trying to preserve his last moments and reconcile what was unfolding before him.

He was fearful of the unknown, of death, of judgment, of chastisement, of association. Sometimes today we find ourselves in similar positions, walking with Christ but denying Him because of the fear that being separate brings, therefore we try to fit in.

With Christ being removed from amongst them, Peter no longer knew who he was. He wanted to be strong. He wanted to be courageous. He wanted to be selfless. But he struggled with self-identity and who he was in Christ.

Throughout Peter's experiences with Christ, he asked Him many questions and those questions would later become the main foundation of his ministry: forgiveness, direction and His deity. Peter wanted to find his identity in Christ, but he first needed the full understanding of who Christ was, so that he could discover who he was.

"And you, that were sometimes alienated and enemies in your mind by wicked works, now yet hath He reconciled." Colossians 1:21

Peter had an experience with Christ. He walked, talked and broke bread with Him. Yet Jesus was able to perceive that *"Satan desired to sift him as wheat."* Luke 18:22

And one of the ways he does this is by trying to put him into bondage by reminding him of his shortcomings and denial of Christ.

Satan is still using the same tactics on us today. However, just as there were occasions that presented themselves for God's glory, through Peter's questioning and fear, we learn how we are supposed to respond in the face of uncertainty, doubt, and fear.

Peter had to deny Christ three times because he had to deal with the very things that were plaguing him and keeping him from a full life in Christ.

He had to deny him three times so that he could take an introspective look at himself and confront the voices that were in his head, keeping him from feeling free.

He had to deny him three times so you and I can understand that there is a process to becoming fully free to walk with Christ, which involves facing those inner things which keep holding us back.

Why?

Because the enemy doesn't care what experiences and encounters we have with Christ, as long as he can plant a seed of fear or doubt in our life. As long as there remains a pending question of His power and sovereignty, the enemy will always try to manipulate the truth and have us second guess what we know to be true.

We have to believe that:

In spite of what's going on around us, in us and outside of us, we need to ask God to keep our hearts pure, bless us, and enlarge our territory to help us keep going forward and gaining ground for Him.

What we speak and what we say takes root not only in our hearts and in our minds, so that we can believe what we claim, for *"Out of the abundance of our heart the mouth speaks."* Luke 6:45

The things that we think are going to manifest in the way that we live and speak and believe *"For as a man thinketh so is he ..."* Proverbs 23:7

God favors those who ask and earnestly want His will to be fulfilled and see His manifestation.

So, what is on the other side?

On this side of victory is gain. On the other side of victory, is defeat.

On this side of joy is peace. On the other side of joy, is sorrow.

On this side of certainty is trust. On the other side of certainty, is doubt.

On this side of praise is possession. On the other side of praise, is depression.

On this side of confidence is faith. On the other side of confidence, is fear.

On this side of hope is fulfillment. On the other side of hope, is emptiness.

On this side of Christ is life. On the other side of Christ, is death.

"If God be for you, who (what, where, when, why, how) *can* (anything, anyone, anywhere) *be against you?"* Romans 8:31

What are the things in your life that are causing you to deny Christ?

What are the things hindering your faith?

What are the internal struggles you wrestle with that make you question who you are in Him?

Before the cock crow and the sun rises on a new day, make sure you begin to confront the things that the enemy is trying to impute on you to make you deny Him, so that they can be dispelled.

Confront the lies, doubts and fears that keep you from possessing full freedom and life in Him. And do not trade in what you have on this side for what's on the other side.

My friends and fellow brethren know this, we are already equipped and endowed with everything we need to tear down the gates of hell and overcome the struggles that inhibit us from being the powerhouse that we were called to be.

Look at the miracles, signs and wonders we currently are, and contemplate the things we have witnessed, experienced and done in our journey thus far, despite our weaknesses, reasonings and shortcomings.

We have been made a promise and that promise will be fulfilled. He is committed to seeing the work He started in us to the end so that we can become who He intended for us to be before we were even formed in our mother's womb. Philippians 1:6, Jeremiah 29:11

Therefore, when you and I are able to operate in full faith, excavating our hearts from the things that hinder us, such as doubt, fear, self-dependency, rationalization and rejection, we will be a force to be reckoned with in the kingdom of God.

"For I will give you a mouth and wisdom which all your adversaries shall not be able to gainsay nor resist." Luke 21:15

Father, Direct Me

Heavenly Father, I come before you knowing that You are the perfect parent all encompassed into one.

Before You formed me in my mother's womb You knew me, and before I was born You chose me and consecrated me; You know my beginning from my ending and all the parts in between And still You love me You know the plans that you have for my life, plans to prosper me and give me a hope and a future.

You called me for greatness and desire the best outcome for my life.

Lord, forgive me for sometimes forgetting that You're ordering my steps.

That I was bought with a price and I am not my own.

Remind me that You are my shepherd and I am the sheep of Your pasture.

Lead me and help me to follow.

You are a protector of Your sheep You keep them safeguarded.

Without You, they are lost and in a state of confusion and can easily be led astray.

But as the good Shepherd and Father, You lead us and guide us into all truths, You protect us from dangers and snares both aware and unaware.

Father, Your intended purpose is to bring me to a still quiet place where I can hear from You and know Your will for my life.

Replenish my soul and quench my thirst.

Lord, help me to remember that as long as I follow, You're leading, I will never want for any good thing, because all that I need is in You, and You will ensure that I have what I need to accomplish my purpose in You.

You love me Father and You're dedicated to seeing me through until I have fulfilled my destiny, which Is why You were willing to sacrifice Your son Jesus Christ my Lord and savior for my life.

You know what's best for me.

You said no good thing will You withhold from them that love You.

So, if I seem to lack anything, it is not Your will for me because in You I lack nothing.

I thank you Father that Your love for me is so vast I could never imagine or confine it to the small thinking of my mind.

I ask that You direct me so that I may follow, and If I go astray, please redirect me because only You know what is best for me.

Father, I trust You.

Father, I trust You.

Father, I trust You.

You are the perfect parent and You care for Your children well.

Amen.

www.ingramcontent.com/pod-product-compliance
Lightning Source LLC
Chambersburg PA
CBHW061304110426
42742CB00012BA/2055